A(ZX)103

An Introduction to the Humanities

The Open University

Form and Reading

Block 1

This publication forms part of an Open University course A(ZX)103 *An Introduction to the Humanities*. Details of this and other Open University courses can be obtained from the Student Registration and Enquiry Service, The Open University, PO Box 197, Milton Keynes, MK7 6BJ, United Kingdom: tel.+44 (0)870 333 4340, email general-enquiries@open.ac.uk

Alternatively, you may visit the Open University website at http://www.open.ac.uk where you can learn more about the wide range of courses and packs offered at all levels by The Open University

To purchase a selection of Open University course materials visit http://www.open.ac.uk, or contact Open University Worldwide, Michael Young Building, Walton Hall, Milton Keynes MK7 6AA, United Kingdom for a brochure. tel. +44 (0)1908 858785; fax +44 (0)1908 858787; e-mail ouwenq@open.ac.uk

The Open University
Walton Hall, Milton Keynes
MK7 6AA

First published 1997. Second edition 2005.

Edited and designed by The Open University.

Typeset by The Open University.

Printed and bound in the United Kingdom by Scotprint.

ISBN 0 7492 9663 1

2.1

31612B/a103b1i2.1

INTRODUCTION TO BLOCK 1

Written for the course team by Charles Harrison

If you have been working through the A103 preparatory material, you will already have an idea of the ground covered by the Arts disciplines. In the four units of this block you will be focusing on the specific disciplines of art (Unit 1), literature (Unit 2), music (Unit 3) and philosophy (Unit 4), and practising the particular activities and skills associated with each – looking, reading, listening and reasoning. The divisions between these skills should not be taken too literally, however. In responding to the arts, we draw both on our reasoning abilities and on our senses in various combinations. And, as will have been clear from your work on the theme of war memorials in the preparatory material, there is considerable overlap among the various disciplines.

It is primarily in art, literature and music that we expect what we normally think of as works of art. You will be introduced to representative examples in Units 1–3. That we refer to *works* of art is a reminder that such things as paintings, poems and musical compositions result from the practical activities undertaken by artists, writers and composers. We aim in this block to help you to understand the kinds of materials and techniques with which works of art are made, to give you some experience and guidance in analysing their forms, and to enable you to explore the distinctive pleasures they offer. TV1, *Framing and Forming*, is specifically concerned with the art of painting, but it also raises issues relevant to the block as a whole.

'Form' is a key concept here. Anything we single out for attention must have a form of some kind – otherwise how could it be singled out? Thus we speak of natural forms, such as rocks or trees, but also of forms of behaviour or forms of argument, the last of these being a particular concern of philosophy. In fact, what gives the term a special place both in philosophy and in discussions of the arts is that the kinds of form at issue are those in which human meanings and intentions are expressed. The one factor uniting the different components of this block, therefore, is a concern with the relationship between form and meaning.

We have to be a little careful here. We can say with confidence that this relationship lies at the heart of painting, of poetry, of music and of philosophical argument alike. But if we try to analyse how this relationship works, we will have to proceed in different ways according to the different types of form involved. In other words, learning to 'read' a piece of music or a painting requires skills that differ in significant respects from those we employ in the reading of a poem. The 'meaning' we may find in a piece of music or in a painting is a different *kind* of meaning from that which is carried by a philosophical statement or even a poem, and it is carried in a different way. One important difference is that philosophical statements and poems use verbal language, whereas music and painting do not.

You will find that the four units in this block have different numbers of pages, though in fact the actual work you have to do is roughly the same in each week. Thus Unit 1, on art, is the longest of the four – but you don't have to do any additional reading. The literature unit (Unit 2) is of medium length, and requires you to read a number of sonnets in *Resource Book 1* – in addition to those printed in the unit itself. Unit 3, on music, is also of medium length, which gives you time for the listening exercises. The philosophy unit has been kept short so that you can devote sufficient time to the accompanying exercises; these have been designed to give you practice in distinguishing between valid and invalid arguments.

Note: all the units in Block 1 contain brief marginal references to *The Arts Good Study Guide*, with which you will already be familiar if you have been working through the preparatory material. These references indicate parts of the guide that give advice about relevant study procedures; follow them up in cases where you would like further support.

UNIT 1   SEEING

Written for the course team by Charles Harrison

Contents

STUDY WEEK ONE

STUDY COMPONENTS				
Weeks of study	Texts	TV	AC	Set books
1	*Illustration Book*	TV1	AC1, Band 1	–

Aims and objectives

The aims of this unit are:

1   to interest you in painting, and introduce you to some distinguished examples of the art;

2   to describe some basic characteristics of pictures, and to show how some conventional forms of pictorial composition and illusion work in practice;

3   through guided comparison, to demonstrate a range of typical painterly effects;

4   to help you learn, through comparison, how to observe the significant features of different works and different styles;

5   to encourage thought about the usefulness and relevance of biographical and other information in understanding works of art;

6   to introduce the concept of iconography and to raise some preliminary questions about the uses and limitations of iconographical approaches;

7   to consider the role of the spectator in responding to pictorial composition, using Rembrandt's *The Artist in his Studio* as a case study.

By the end of this unit you should be able:

1   to provide a brief and accurate description of a conventional type of painting, making relevant observations on the treatment of light and shade and on the organization of pictorial space;

2   to make distinctions between comparable paintings in terms of technique, treatment of subject and compositional effects;

3   when considering the form of a work of art, to exercise suitable caution over the relevance of biographical information;

4   to provide at least one example of a pictorial form used to convey a specific symbolic meaning;

5   when faced with a traditional type of pictorial composition, to give some account of its effect in structuring the imaginative experience of the spectator;

6   to visit a picture gallery or museum of art with enhanced understanding and enjoyment of the work on display;

7   to communicate some part of that understanding and enjoyment to others.

Pronunciation guide

The italic text below gives an idea of how to pronounce the names of artists referred to in Unit 1. Where we place an accent in the italics, it means that, when the name is pronounced, this syllable should be stressed:

Sandro Botticelli (Italian): *Sandro Bottichélli*

Gustave Courbet (French): *Goostav Korbay*

Edgar Degas (French): *Edgar Degáh*

Eugène Delacroix (French): *Erjayn Déllacrwah*

Domenico Veneziano (Italian): *Dohménnyko Vennaytziáno*

Gerard Dou (Dutch): *Gherrad Dow*

Albrecht Dürer (German): *Allbresht Dyoora*

Giovanni di Paolo (Italian): *Jováni di Powlo*

Louise Moillon (French): *Looeez Mwulloh*

Claude Monet (French): *Clode Monnay*

Piero della Francesca (Italian): *Pee-airo della Franchéska*

Rembrandt van Rijn (Dutch): *Rembrant van Rin (he is usually just known as Rembrandt)*

Hans Vredeman de Vries (Dutch): *Fraydeman der Frees*

Names not listed are pronounced as written.

The artists: dates of birth and death

Sandro Botticelli: 1444/5–1510

Frederick Church: 1826–1900

John Constable: 1776–1837

Gustave Courbet: 1819–77

Edgar Degas: 1834–1917

Eugène Delacroix: 1798–1863

Domenico Veneziano: active 1438–61

Gerard Dou: 1613–75

Albrecht Dürer: 1471–1528

Giovanni di Paolo: *c.*1399–1482

Jan Davidsz de Heem: 1606–83/4

Jacques Linard: *c.*1600–45

Louise Moillon: 1610–96

Claude Monet: 1840–1926

Barnett Newman: 1905–70

(Sir) William Nicholson: 1872–1949

Piero della Francesca: *c.*1415–92

Rembrandt van Rijn: 1606–69

John Russell: 1745–1806

Jan Steen: 1625/6–79

Harmen Steenwyck: 1612–after 1655

Adriaen van Utrecht: 1599–1652

Otto van Veen: 1556–1629

Daniel Vosmaer: 1622–after 1666

Hans Vredeman de Vries: 1527–?1606

Joseph Wright of Derby: 1734–97

A note on the reading of captions

When we print a reproduction of a painting, or other work of art, we nearly always provide a full caption as well. For example:

Colour Plate 1   Rembrandt van Rijn, The Artist in his Studio, c.1629, oil on panel, 25 x 32 cm. Museum of Fine Arts, Boston, accession no.38.1838

This gives you a great deal of useful information, not just the artist's name and the title of the work, but also the date when it was painted – in this case roughly 1629 (the *c.* before a date stands for *circa*, Latin for 'about'). The caption will tell you whether the artist used oil, pastel, etc., what surface he or she painted on (wood panel in this case, though it might be canvas, paper, etc.), and what its dimensions are. Read this information carefully, because it will give you clues about the work. The final piece of information is the name of the gallery or other collection where the work is to be found.

Having said that the information is useful, I want to warn you about titles. Of course they can be helpful in telling you what it is you should be seeing, but bear in mind that the title by which a work of art becomes known was not necessarily given it by the artist. Where a date is given, ask yourself whether the title is one that is likely to have been used at the time in question. The older the work, the less likely the title is to be original and the more likely it is to be the product of later interpretation.

what is the was painted with + what it was painted on.

Information about medium will help you to imagine the effect of the original work. This effect will depend in part on the physical form of the work and on the function for which it was intended. All other things being equal, works on paper tend to be less expensive both to make and to buy than works on canvas or wood. Artists will often use pencil, ink or crayon on paper to try out ideas and details before working them up in the more expensive medium of oil on canvas or wood. Pastels are soft and chalky crayons. Used on paper they produce a delicate and vulnerable surface with subtle colour effects. Oil paints have been used since the fifteenth century. Because they can be mixed to different consistencies, they allow the artist to choose from a wide range of surface effects – from very smooth and fine, to thick and textured. They are also slow-drying, which allows the artist time to revise his or her work. Once dry, the surface of an oil painting is relatively durable. Tempera was widely used by artists in Italy before the introduction of oil paints. In this case the pigment – the substance giving the colour – is mixed not with oil but with egg, the white being used for lighter colours and transparent effects, and the yolk to add density and warmth. Tempera is a less fluid and flexible medium than oil. It tends to dry faster and demands an even application and a light touch. In the hands of a skilled technician, tempera can be used to produce a coloured surface of great clarity and brilliance.

Information about size should be read in connection with information about medium. Clearly an oil painting small enough to be carried in a briefcase is a very different kind of thing from a mural occupying an entire wall. When reproduced in a book, however, they might appear the same size. In the absence of a full caption it might not even be clear that one was a portable object painted on canvas while the other was painted directly onto the wall. Where such information *is* given, you can often make use of it: for example, a small oil painting is likely to have been produced for a private purpose – as a sketch for the artist's own use, as a commission from someone whose reasons were largely personal, or for speculative sale to a buyer who would not have had to be very wealthy. A work too large to have been easily carried is more likely to have been commissioned for some public purpose, as a form of commemoration, for state or civic propaganda, or in order to embody religious meanings and values. If you keep these points in mind, they will help you interpret the image you are looking at.

Information about the location of a work may also have much to tell you if you give it some thought. A work in the collection of a museum is rarely in the place for which it was designed. This in itself should give you pause for thought. Trying to imagine its original function is a useful way to start inquiring into a work of art. A still life might have been intended to decorate a private dining room or study, a portrait to hang in a family home. The great majority of paintings on religious themes were intended for devotional purposes. Many of them were commissioned for specific churches or chapels. As we shall see, many of the small Italian pictures now in the world's richest museums are actually fragments long separated from much larger altarpieces. On the other hand, if the caption tells you that the work in question is to be found in a church, there is a chance that it is still in the position it was designed for. It is thus more likely to be in its original form – though you should bear in mind that a work of art that appears to have survived intact for centuries may actually have been adapted at some point to serve a different purpose, to fit a different space or frame, or simply in response to changes in taste and fashion. Remember that reproductions have the effect of *reducing* differences between works of art, of *obscuring* their practical aspects, and of *masking* their complex histories.

CASSETTE 1, SIDE 1, BAND 1

This would be a good point at which to listen to AC1, Band 1, 'Art history', which offers advice about getting the most out of looking at works of art in museums and galleries.

1   INTRODUCTION

We will start this unit with a picture. Please look at Colour Plate 1 (the first in the *Illustration Book*). This is by one of the most famous painters in the history of art, the Dutch artist Rembrandt van Rijn (usually just known as Rembrandt). It was painted around 1629, when he was about twenty-three years old. It now hangs in the Museum of Fine Arts in Boston, Massachusetts.

EXERCISE

For this exercise, write down some comments on the painting. First, describe what you think the picture shows, using not more than one hundred words. Then, in not more than fifty words, try to describe its effect on you. Lastly, say whether or not you like the work, giving brief reasons if you can.

DISCUSSION

We will return to this painting at the end of the unit, when we will look at it more closely. By then I hope that various things will have happened. The first is that you will know more about the skills required to compose and to produce such an image. The second is that you will have a better sense of the richness of meaning that even so small and apparently simple an image can convey. And the third is that you will be better able to explain, to yourself and to others, why a little painted rectangle such as this should be held in such high esteem. So if, at the end of the unit, you come back to what you wrote for this activity, you should find it easy to add to – or change – your notes under the first two headings.

Whether you change what you have written under the third heading is another matter, and will depend in part on what you have said. But I would like to make clear that there is no failure involved in not *liking* a work of art, whether it is a painting, a poem, or a piece of music, however authoritative its admirers may appear and however wonderful they may take it to be. We fail in the encounter with works of art only if we refuse to look or to read or to listen. But the looking I have in mind does require a certain level or *quality* of attention (as we might give the best rather than the least of our attention to another person). As I aim to show, there may be more to look for and to look at than is immediately apparent in a painting such as Rembrandt's *The Artist in his Studio.*

---

2 FORM AND SPACE IN PAINTING

In this first unit we shall be looking at a range of paintings, drawn from various phases of the Western artistic tradition, from the fifteenth century to the twentieth. I want to start by establishing some basic points about the way in which pictures have been understood and thought about within that tradition, and about the means by which pictures have typically been made to *work* for their spectators. Think of this as an introduction to the grammar of painting: that's to say, to the ways in which parts are related to each other so as to compose meaningful wholes. In the later sections we will be looking at some more complex pictures. As we work through the unit I hope to demonstrate how rich a medium of expression painting can be. You will not be expected to look at all the plates in detail. Some of them are there to provide points of amplification or comparison for the main works under discussion, and some may be revisited later in the course at summer school or in connection with tutor-marked assignments. (The note in the margin on this page is a reminder that, if you would like it, help is available in *The Arts Good Study Guide.*)

AGSG, ch.6, sect.5, 'Evaluation'

Before we proceed I want to establish some basic points about the relationship between images and words, pictures and verbal language. We might say that both the painter and the writer normally start off with a flat surface, and that both mark that surface so that it will be understood as having content of a sort – that's to say, so that it will be understood as referring to something. But here we encounter an important difference. The elements of writing – words – refer to their objects by custom and convention, rather than by being *like* them. The word 'cat' neither resembles a cat nor sounds like a cat. To call something a picture of a cat, on the other hand, is to say that it refers to a cat *because it resembles one.* Look now at Colour Plate 2 and Plates 1 and 2. These are a landscape by a nineteenth-century American painter, a group portrait by a Flemish artist and a still life by an English painter working in the early part of the twentieth century. Think for a moment about what these pictures show, and consider what it would be like to provide some equivalents for them in writing. If I try to imagine such a task I feel instantly daunted by the time it would take – the endless sequences of words I would have to string one after another. And as I imagine those sequences, I think of the loss there would be – a loss of immediacy. However painstaking my writing, it could never capture the *look* of evening light as Church's picture does. And the more fully I describe all the people in van Veen's picture or all the jugs in Nicholson's, the further away I would be moving from the distinctive experience their pictures provide – that of seeing relationship and variety *simultaneously* displayed.

There are some important lessons to be drawn. Pictures may not be particularly suitable for conveying the kinds of information that are most easily absorbed sequentially, like narratives and reports. But where what we wish to convey are observable qualities and relations – impressions and effects, similarities and differences – then pictures come into their own. And this is principally because, whereas the meanings of verbal language are built up in linear sequences (over time), a picture – within the Western tradition at least – is something that can usually be seen all at once. As a viewer, you may need time to take it all in, but this is not because it unfolds over time like a speech, or has to be read in order like a piece of writing. When we think of what it means to compose a picture, then, what we are considering are the techniques used by artists to make something we can look *at* and look *into*. These are the kinds of techniques we shall be exploring in this unit.

To summarize: to make a picture is to do something to a flat surface with the intention that the surface will be viewed as having a form of content. This content is of a special kind: (a) it is decided by what the marked surface *looks like*; (b) it is all present at once (even though it may take the viewer some time to explore). I put the matter in this way because I want to make the point that the very *first* condition for the making of a picture is not the composing of a likeness, however basic that likeness may be. What must come first is the *idea* that a likeness is something a flat surface can be made to contain.

Now there are some kinds of likeness that can be produced without altering our sense of a surface *as* flat. To return to our comparison with writing, if I draw a letter 'A' on one sheet and copy it onto another, the second 'A' is a likeness of the first and it has been achieved without the aid of any illusion of depth. In fact, of course, you would be justified in saying that I am not really making a picture – not 'drawing' at all. What I am actually doing is 'writing', albeit at a very basic level. We might say that it is only once we get past this very simple kind of similarity – the likeness of one 'A' to another 'A' – that the special *value* of pictures is realized. Another way to put this would be to say that it is only once pictures start to do what writing *can't* do that they start to be interesting and useful. In this sense, even a crude drawing of a stick person represents a considerable advance on the letter 'A', though it may not be much harder to make.

There are two reasons for this, and they are inextricably connected. The first is this: unlike the letter 'A', which needs only to be identifiable as an

'A' in order to perform its function, the stick person pictures – or is 'like' – something else. In a very basic sense it is like a human figure. The second reason for the difference between the stick drawing and the letter is that if the stick drawing refers to an actual figure – which is a solid thing, with weight and volume and colour and so on – then the surrounding paper must refer to a space in which that figure notionally exists. The paper you write on remains a flat piece of paper. The paper you draw on becomes an imaginative world.

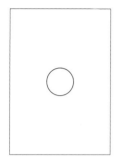

FIGURE 1.1

FIGURE 1.2

EXERCISE

Try a simple experiment for yourself. Draw a circle in the centre of a sheet of paper, like a large capital O, as in Figure 1.1.

Now shade one side of the O, as in Figure 1.2.

DISCUSSION

What you have done is to add *tone* to your drawing. Tone is a quantity of greyness or darkness. The 'tonal range' of a picture is the range from its whitest white to its darkest black. In shading the circle, you have in effect first *imagined* the circle as a sphere, and then signalled this by giving the sphere a dark side and a brightly lit side. In other words you have implied the existence of a source of light. It is light that allows us visually to perceive things in the world and to measure the relations between them. So what is the *effect* of what you have done? It is not just that the circle has ceased to be like a capital O and has become like a sphere. The point is that while a flat sheet of paper can contain a capital O, it cannot contain a sphere. Therefore, since the circle is now seen as a sphere, *something must also have happened to the sheet of paper.* If you can see the shaded circle as a sphere, it must follow that you can see – or *imagine* – the paper as having a 'depth' sufficient to contain it; or rather you must be able to 'see' the ground on which the shaded O is drawn not as a sheet of paper at all, but as if it were a spatial volume sufficient to contain a sphere. Of course you still know that it *is* a sheet of paper, and that it *is* flat. But it is as if your mind has agreed to entertain the illusion that it is something else, in order to make sense of the 'seeing' of the sphere. What has happened, in fact, is that you have exercised imagination.

I suggest that the ability to draw someone into this agreement is the basic condition required to make illusion do its work in painting. I would also like to suggest that the establishment of such agreement is the starting-point for art considered as a *social* activity. The form of social activity I mean to indicate is the relationship of collaboration and of mutual recognition that is established, via the work of art, between the artist who furnishes material for the exercise of imagination, and the spectator willing to undertake the relevant imaginative work. A work of art is like a game – often a very serious game – that is set in play when the spectator's imagination engages according to its rules. Once that point of agreement is reached, endless possibilities are opened up for enriching the illusion and for the consequent enlargement of the picture's possible field of reference. Colour Plate 3 shows a slightly more complex picture of an illuminated sphere (John Russell, *The Face of the Moon*). At first glance you may have taken it for a photograph. In fact this image of the moon was drawn in pastel some decades before the invention of photography, by an artist who must have used a telescope. Again, as a measure of the importance of pictures, try to imagine what it would have been like to convey that information in words.

There is a point to be noted here. It is not *simply* illusion that the spectator assents to or agrees to entertain. It is not just the apparent transformation of the sheet of paper into a space with a sphere in it that holds our attention in such pictures as Russell's. Rather what is intriguing is the curiously paradoxical experience of seeing the paper as both literally flat and imaginatively fathomless. What the art of painting caters to is not simply a taste for illusion, then. Instead, it makes its meaning within the *relationship* between the seeing of the flat painted surface, and the seeing of that surface *as* something else, something much more, something which has been *made* to be as it is.

Like your own shaded sphere, Russell's picture demonstrates a basic figure–ground relationship. Figure–ground relations involve seeing some object both as distinct and as located in a context by which its identity and meaning are established. A black stain on a white sheet draws attention to itself *as* a stain precisely because of its difference from the surrounding area. A solitary post driven into a level field would draw the eye by virtue of its singularity and its uprightness. These may seem like purely formal matters. But figure–ground relations affect how we see things in a more than literal sense. If I call to mind a particular colleague, I am considering that person against the background of an institution of which we are both members. I am likely to be seeing her in the light of a certain working relationship, good or bad. To consider the same person as a member of her family, however, is to accord her a different form of identity, to see her as a figure set against a different ground, in which she is involved in different kinds of relationship with other people.

To take another example: I may worry over the size of a bill if the sum almost matches the total I have in my bank account. Against that background the figure looms large. But if I won the Lottery, the significance of the sum would be reduced – as would my anxiety. Such figure–ground relations are in general crucial to the organization of our thoughts and priorities. By such means we isolate an object of attention against the background of our concerns and preoccupations, so as to give a critical meaning to the relations between them. The meaning is 'critical' in the sense that it raises the issue of relative *values* or significance. In the case of Russell's picture, the image of the moon is built up with great care. Its isolation in the velvety space suggests that it is *worth* looking at – that it is a *significant* object of attention.

In the case of our various spheres, it is clear enough, I think, which part of the picture serves as the figure and which the ground (I would have said 'background', but in this case the spatial grounds extend *in front* of the spheres as well as behind them). But figure–ground relations appear in many different ways in art. Look at Plate 3 (Barnett Newman, untitled drawing: also known as *The Void*), which seems at first glance to show another sphere. In fact, the reference to the void suggests a different reading. It is important, however, that the 'void' is sphere-shaped – or to put it another way, it is significant that the artist has both aroused and reversed our normal expectation that a 'ground' will surround a 'figure'. It is the shock of this reversal that produces the effect of the picture. What we have is a void in place of a sphere, as if the very medium of 'seeing' – or light – had come before there was any object for it to illuminate. The first book of the Bible, the Book of Genesis, opens with the words, 'God created the heaven and the earth. And the earth was without form and void, and darkness was upon the face of the deep.' What Newman's work suggests is that, for the painter, creation begins not with formless matter, but with the command, 'Let there be light'. Once there is light, we can begin to make out figures against grounds, and to distinguish *form* from chaos.

Newman's is a modern picture, of course. Modern artists of his generation were fascinated with the idea of going back to the – or a – 'beginning', and they associated the beginning of creative activity with the kind of 'beginning' of drawing that we have been undertaking so far. At the very end of the course, we shall be looking at the work of Newman's one-time friend and contemporary, Mark Rothko. For now, my point in using this example, and in contrasting it with Russell's picture, is to show that much of the effect of paintings depends not upon the details of what they picture, but rather upon the way that their spaces and surfaces are ordered, and upon the ways in which the spectator can be made to respond to that ordering. We are going to explore this in the next section.

3 PERSPECTIVE

At this point, I would like you to return to your drawing of the sphere.

Draw another sphere, higher up on the same sheet of paper. Imagine that this second sphere is actually the same size as the first, but that it is further away. Try to shade it so that it looks as if it is lit from the same light source as the first sphere.

DISCUSSION

You may well have drawn the second sphere smaller than the first, rather as in Figure 1.3.

FIGURE 1.3

FIGURE 1.4

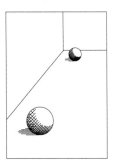

FIGURE 1.5

Now, here is a problem. What if someone fails to see this as a picture of two same-sized spheres, with one nearer than the other? What if he or she insists that it shows a large and small sphere, each the same distance away from the viewer? Your awkward spectator is 'seeing' the two spheres as both located on the same vertical plane – a plane parallel to the literal plane of the paper. The spectator is seeing them as in Figure 1.4.

(Can you see how the surface on which the spheres rest appears as if upright, and thus parallel to the actual page?) What I have done in Figure 1.4 is add in some visual cues to show how the relationship between the spheres is being conceived. Now you want to change your spectator's angle of vision so that the two spheres are seen to lie along a plane that *recedes into the depth* of your picture, so that one is further away than the other. How are you to do it? The answer is to add some different cues of your own, as in Figure 1.5.

Notice that the pairs of spheres in Figures 1.3, 1.4 and 1.5 are all drawn in exactly the same way. What I have done in Figure 1.5 is suggest a basic perspective in order to direct the viewer's vision, so that it appears as if the sphere on the left is seen 'first' as the eye travels into the picture. It seems that we may after all need sequence of a kind in the reading of pictures. It is a sequence, however, which leads us as it were *into* the imaginary space of the picture rather than *across* the literal surface of the paper. Once this perspective is established, if I want to go further and to suggest an actual size for the spheres, I can provide a clue whereby the spectator will be encouraged to relate them to his or her own dimensions, as in Figure 1.6 overleaf.

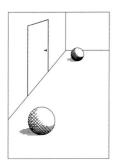

FIGURE 1.6

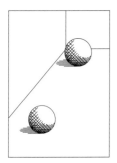

FIGURE 1.7

Now look at Colour Plates 4 and 5 (Giovanni di Paolo, *St John the Baptist going into the Wilderness*; Piero della Francesca, *The Flagellation of Christ*). Both pictures were made by artists working in Italy during the Renaissance in the fifteenth century, when the great majority of paintings were devoted to religious themes. From our modern point of view it seems that, whether he knew it or not, Giovanni di Paolo had a problem which is not unconnected to the one I posed with the two spheres. For most of the picture he has used a basic system of perspective to suggest a gradually increasing depth of space. Thus the small houses in the centre appear much further 'in' than the building that John the Baptist is leaving at the left. But the artist also wants to make the point that the saint has left home and travelled into the mountains, so he shows him twice, after the manner of a strip cartoon. And in order that we'll *know* we are seeing the same person both times, he gives him the same pose and dimensions. The result is that we are faced with two inconsistent cues for measuring the depth of the pictorial space and the relative sizes of the objects within it. Clearly the 'second' John the Baptist would have a severe problem getting into either of the houses in the middle distance. It is as if I had drawn our two spheres literally the same size, while also suggesting that one was further away than the other, as in Figure 1.7.

If you now look at Colour Plate 5, you will find all in order, at least in terms of the coherence of its pictorial space. This shows the flagellation of Christ in the presence of Pontius Pilate, with three mysterious figures in the foreground who seem to be conducting a kind of conversation about the meaning of the event. Where Giovanni di Paolo, the painter of the first picture, conveyed the sense of distance by dramatic changes of scale and by atmospheric effects, Piero della Francesca creates the illusion of a measured progress into depth across a level urban space. This space is complicated by the presence of a series of buildings. These are so clearly delineated that you might assume the artist had drawn them from life. In fact it is more likely that he designed them for the purposes of his picture.

Think for a moment about what this means. If he did not actually make models of these buildings, then he must have *imagined* them on a geometrical basis, no doubt using a ground-plan to help him work out their placing and proportions so that they would look right when seen in perspective from the intended viewpoint. Plate 4 shows a reconstruction of the ground-plan of his picture, produced by a modern architect working with an art historian. (A ground-plan is a bird's-eye view, used to map out the horizontal areas occupied by forms such as buildings, and to specify the distances between them.) Notice how large a space the artist has had to plan in order to produce the effect the perspective achieves. Unlike Giovanni di Paolo, Piero was in possession of the geometrical and mathematical skills that enabled him both to work out such a plan and its accompanying elevation (the head-on perpendicular view of the buildings) and then to translate these into a picture.

The system he used is that of single-point perspective, which was first developed by artists and architects in Italy working earlier in the fifteenth century. A *system* of perspective is a consistent means of translating three dimensions into two. In the particular system Piero has used, forms which are of equal height in actuality are pictured so that they appear to reduce in even progression according to their distance from the viewer, like the two spheres in Figure 1.3. The 'single point' is the vanishing point on the horizon at which the receding parallel lines joining points of equal height are made to converge. It marks the imaginary deepest point into which the viewer of the picture sees. Here is a simple illustration of such a system at work. I have drawn in the converging lines that an artist would use to establish the perspective, though these would normally be erased or covered over once the initial composition was worked out.

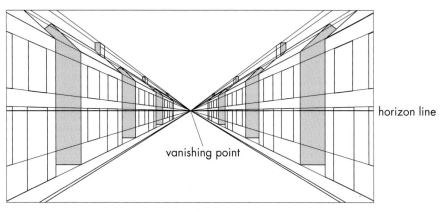

FIGURE 1.8

The vanishing point in Piero's picture is close to the centre of his composition. The effect of this is to give the viewer the impression of being firmly placed on the threshold of the scene and of looking directly into the centre of the proceedings. The height at which the horizon of a picture is set serves to define the horizontal *angle* of the spectator's view into the scene it presents. In this respect, consider the differences between Figures 1.9, 1.10 and 1.11. Notice how changing the height of the horizon affects the sense of distance. Because it changes how it *feels* to be looking, it even affects the imaginary mood of the scene.

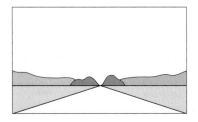

FIGURE 1.9

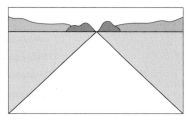

FIGURE 1.10

FIGURE 1.11

EXERCISE

Plates 5, 6 and 7 and 8 provide examples of pictures with eccentric or 'extreme' vanishing points (Edgar Degas, *Miss La La at the Cirque Fernando*; Hans Vredeman de Vries, perspective view; Walt Disney Studios, background drawing; Daniel Vosmaer, *Loggia with a View of Delft*).

See if you can work out where these points are located.

DISCUSSION

In Plate 5 the vanishing point is outside the top of the picture. The artist has provided few clues that would allow it to be pinpointed. What he has done, however, is to create the strong impression that we are craning our necks to look upwards into the picture's illusionistic space. In Plates 6 and 7 the vanishing point is set right at the bottom centre of the picture, creating precisely the opposite effect. In Plate 8 it is set at the extreme left-hand edge. Note what happens in each case to your own assumed position and angle of view. The example from the Disney Studios (Plate 7) is a background drawing for a cartoon film. It serves to make the point that the success of an animated film is not simply a matter of making the figures appear to move. In the hands of the skilful artist, the effect of motion depends at least as much upon the continual reorientation of the spectator's viewpoint, which is achieved by changes of perspective and angle of vision. In the drama of figure–ground relations, our attention will be the more powerfully engaged if the ground is also allowed to move.

There is a final point to be made before we leave the paintings by Giovanni di Paolo and Piero della Francesca. Although the two pictures were painted close in date, I have suggested that Piero was using mathematical and geometrical techniques that Giovanni di Paolo probably did not have. In the mid-fifteenth century the development of such techniques was of great interest to some painters in Italy, though not to all. By giving their pictures the look of systematic organization and truth to appearances, artists such as Piero della Francesca and Leonardo da Vinci were able to raise the intellectual status of painting. What their work seemed to show was that art depended upon forms of theoretical knowledge and understanding, not simply the practising of skills and techniques. If a painting could be seen as something composed in the mind like a poem, and not simply 'made' in the hand like a work of craft, then it was more likely to attract the attention of those who prided themselves on their own literacy and sophistication. In this sense, we might say that Piero's work represents a more advanced state of technical development than Giovanni's, or even that it is more 'modern'.

We should be careful, however. I do not think it automatically follows from this that Piero's is a 'better' painting than Giovanni's. The intellectual achievements of Piero's work are certainly impressive. But they do nothing to disqualify the decorative charm and imaginativeness of Giovanni's. There is no reason to assume that a particular form of technical or intellectual development must involve an increase in artistic quality. A form of organized and systematic 'truth to appearances' is *one* property a painting may have. Decorative charm and individuality are others. These two properties *may* go together, but there is no reason why they should have to. Art-historical treatments of the art of the Italian Renaissance have tended to stress the development of perspective systems – rightly enough, for these developments played a crucial part in shaping the course of art over the next 400 years. But we should not allow this emphasis to blind us to the virtues of such work as Giovanni's: the vividness and homeliness of its detail, the evocative quality of its atmosphere, and its forthright way of showing the passage of time.

Summary

Before you move to Section 4, I will summarize a number of terms that are useful in understanding and analysing pictures. I have already introduced most of them, but one or two are new:

1   First, remember the relationship between lighting and modelling. (In painting, modelling means giving form the appearance of three-dimensionality, or 'plasticity'.) *Shading* a form involves adding *tone* in such a way as to indicate its relation to a *light source* (it will appear lighter on the side from which the light is coming). The *tonal range* of a picture is the range between its lightest light and its darkest dark. Where the tonal range is narrow, as in Colour Plate 6 (Claude Monet, *Ice Floes*), this will tend to convey the impression of an even or subdued lighting and it will consequently reduce effects of modelling. Colour Plate 7, on the other hand, shows the kinds of dramatic pictorial effect that can be produced with sharp light–dark contrasts and a wide overall tonal range (Joseph Wright of Derby, *The Earth-stopper on the Banks of the Derwent*). Notice that the individual forms appear correspondingly solid and distinct from one another.

2   Other terms refer to the organization of illusionistic spaces. A *literal plane* is the actual flat surface of a piece of paper or canvas – the surface you can touch. The *picture plane*, on the other hand, is a surface you cannot touch, though it may seem to correspond to the literal surface of the picture. It is the invisible and imaginary front or nearest level of the picture's illusory space. To place yourself imaginatively up against it is to stand on the threshold of that space. An *illusionistic plane* is a part of the fictional scheme of the

picture. An illusionistic plane may actually be depicted (as in Figure 1.5), or it may simply be implied by the relationship of two or more objects in a picture space (as in Figure 1.3). An *angle of vision* is the plane along which a line of sight is projected into the space of the picture. In many pictures, like the *Portrait of Agatha Bas* shown in Plate 9, the *angle of vision* is set at right angles both to the picture plane and to the literal plane of the picture, suggesting an upright, head-on viewing position for the spectator (the kind of position represented by Figure 1.4 rather than Figure 1.5, for instance). In Piero della Francesca's *Flagellation* (Colour Plate 5) the viewing position is similar to the portrait's, but here the angle of vision is shown as running parallel to the horizontal plane of the ground, so that the spectator who is presumably standing appears to be looking deep into the composition. In the engraving by Vredeman de Vries and the Disney drawing (Plates 6 and 7), on the other hand, the angle of vision is set so that we feel as if we are looking straight downward. This means that it intersects the plane of the horizontal at a right angle. The *perspective* of a picture is a compositional system which serves both to organize the spatial relations between depicted forms, and to define the *angle of vision* of the spectator so that this organization will make sense. Thus the exaggerated perspective of the Disney drawing becomes credible and effective when we adopt in imagination the disconcerting angle of vision that it defines.

Pause here to assess your progress in reading and understanding the unit so far: if you have found it more difficult than you expected, look at AGSG, ch.2, sect.3, 'Reading strategically'

As you become more used to 'reading' pictures with these terms and concepts in mind, you will find that you gain new insights into the ways in which artistic effects are created. The next section will provide you with a detailed exposition of the kinds of analysis involved. You will find that your understanding of pictures will continue to improve if you practise applying the relevant concepts to any pictures you may have to hand, in books or on your walls, or in any galleries or museums you may visit. Try identifying light sources, noting the way forms have been modelled by shading; consider the part played by tonal range and contrast in creating a sense of mood and atmosphere; work out the level of horizons and the location of vanishing points; try to decide the imaginary position in which a picture places you as its spectator and the angle of vision it invites you to adopt; see if you can identify an illusionistic plane which is not actually delineated, but which is defined by the spatial relations between two or more objects.

4 TWO STILL LIFES:
(1) SEEING WHAT, AND SEEING HOW

Please look now at Colour Plates 8 and 9 (Louise Moillon, *Still Life*, c.1630; Gustave Courbet, *Still Life with Apples and Pomegranate*, 1876). These both show oil paintings of the type known as still life.

A NOTE ON THE GENRES OF ART

Still life is one of the 'genres' (French for 'kinds' or 'categories') into which the practice of painting was divided according to the French Academy (a body that was established in the mid-seventeenth century). The authorities of the French Academy did not invent these categories: they simply codified the different types of picture that had emerged in practice over centuries, through processes of interaction between the requirements of religious, civic and individual patrons on the one hand, and developments in artistic techniques and interests on the other. Paintings with moralizing or propagandizing themes drawn from religion, history and literature were gathered under the heading of history painting. This was the most prestigious of the genres, with the most evidently public function, attracting work on the largest scale and requiring the widest range of skills in composition and execution. (We shall be considering history painting further in Block 3 in relation to the work of Jacques Louis David at the time of the French Revolution. For now, note that Plate 11 shows a nineteenth-century example of the genre, Delacroix's *Return of Christopher Columbus* of 1839.) Next in rank was portraiture (see Plates 9 and 10), followed by landscape painting (see Plate 12: John Constable, *Wivenhoe Park, Essex*), the genre of low-life or peasant scenes (confusingly known as '*genre* painting'; see Plate 13, *The Life of Man* by Jan Steen), and finally still life. Landscape and still life were considered as 'low' genres because least suitable for the instilling of moral content – though, as we shall see, paintings in the still-life genre could be rich in their own distinctive kinds of philosophical content, while low-life scenes often carried warnings against the dangers of idleness or drunkenness or sexual licence. The theory of the genres remained a powerful means of classification and organization of the practice of painting for the next 250 years, and its influence is still felt today.

In the traditional language of the art school and the studio, a painting 'from life' is one that depends upon the study of an object that the artist has actually available to view, typically a model posed for the purpose. Such paintings are contrasted with those, like Plate 11, which are *composed* from imagination and in that sense invented, though their individual forms and details may be based on 'life study', and though their subjects may be derived from historical or literary texts. A 'still' subject is one that can be counted on not to move. Thus a typical 'still life' is a picture showing objects which we assume to have been real and present to the painter, and that are inanimate. The French term for still life is *nature morte*, literally 'dead nature', or 'inert nature'. A painting of a landscape might include a representation of a swan (Plate 12). The same bird laid out dead on a table becomes a suitable object for inclusion in an opulent still life (see Plate 14, Adriaen van Utrecht, *Still Life with White Swan*).

EXERCISE

Look carefully at the reproductions of still lifes by Moillon and Courbet (Colour Plates 8 and 9). How are they similar in terms of subject-matter, composition, lighting and so on? How are they different?

You should expect to write 150–200 words in note form, and to spend about half an hour on this exercise. After you have read to the end of Section 6, I shall invite you to check back over what you have written.

DISCUSSION

Under similarities you may have noted the following: there is a table-top – or similar surface – shown in both paintings; both include centrepieces of edible fruit; in both cases some of the still-life materials have been placed directly on the table-top as if there had been too much for their respective containers; and in both cases the background is dark and indefinite. These are all statements about *what* is pictured. You might have gone a bit further to consider *how* these elements are made to work in the paintings. Thus in each case the table-top is seen at an angle that suggests a viewpoint slightly above and quite close to, so that we have a downward-slanting angle of vision; in both the fruit is positioned close to the picture plane or 'front' of the composition, as if within reach, while much is made of its colour and texture; in both cases the light seems to fall on the fruit from the left foreground, while the dark background serves to set the various objects into relief and to concentrate our attention upon them. In both pictures there is a relatively wide tonal range.

I describe this second series of common features as ways in which the components of the picture are 'made to work'. Thus we progress from describing *what* is pictured to noticing *how* the picturing is done. This is an important development, for what then becomes clear is that it is done in such a way as to produce a series of *effects* – ways in which we, as spectators, are drawn to respond imaginatively to the paintings. It is only when our imagination is set to work that they really come alive for us. But note that this imaginative activity is not free-ranging: in both cases the composition has been formed and organized so that quite specific effects – feelings of nearness, of concentration, and of stimulation of the sense of touch – are the effects that will be produced in the attentive viewer.

We have seen that the two paintings have much in common but, when it comes to considering the differences, there are actually so many that it is hard to pin them down to a straightforward list. It may help if we establish some categories.

First of all, differences in the objects pictured. Moillon's painting shows a basket full of fruit – a fine basket full of fine fruits, with the bloom of ripeness upon them. Courbet's painting shows a plate piled with apples and a single pomegranate. The plate is a piece of rustic pottery, chipped with use, and though the apples are glowing with colour they are also scabby and bruised – windfalls perhaps. Moillon includes a bundle of asparagus at the front right and some leaves (and pods?) at the front left, Courbet a pewter jug and a glass with some liquid (wine? beer? cider?) further back at the left. It is also noticeable that Moillon shows us the front edge of her table, whereas in Courbet's painting the surface continues forward as it were past the picture plane and into the spectator's own space.

Secondly, differences in the way the picturing is done. (This category includes differences in style and technique.) The fineness of Moillon's fruit is in part conveyed by a refined manner of painting. Everything is smoothly and carefully delineated, with attention to detail and to the subtle gradations of surface and texture. Notice particularly how the soft and gradual transition from light to shade on the peaches and plums contributes to the illusion of their roundness. Although various textures are represented in the painting, its literal surface retains a glassy smoothness overall. By contrast, Courbet's painting presents a rougher and more variegated surface to the eye, although the painter uses a much narrower range of colours than Moillon. The brushwork on the apples, in particular, looks quite casual or sketchy. (The points made here should be discernible from the reproductions, though of course you could expect them to be much more evident if you were in front of the actual paintings.)

Thirdly, differences in effect. As with the similarities, these are *consequences* of the ways in which the picturing has been done. Thus while the finer technique of the Moillon creates the effect of a sharp light upon the fruit and of an even focus on the part of the observer, the effect of Courbet's glowing colours and more blurred manner is to make us feel as if the apples themselves were radiating warmth and subdued light.

I mentioned earlier that the fruit in both pictures is painted 'as if within reach'. These paintings both offer clear examples of compositional devices – ways in which the painters have organized the forms of their pictures – that serve to prompt the spectator's imagination into an appropriate kind of response. In both cases the subject is presented as if viewed from a specific position (almost on a level and close enough to touch); in both a certain atmosphere is created (relatively dark but with a single light source to the left of the angle of vision); both define a principal object of attention (the pile of fruit); and each seems to convey something that we might call a particular disposition or *mode* of attention (the *manner* in which the various objects are seen or experienced). Courbet's painting, however, sets us closer to the fruit than Moillon's – more nearly on the same level, as if we were leaning our weight upon the same surface.

These considerations lead us to our last form of difference between the two paintings – a difference in what we might call *emotional or expressive quality*. I believe it is the most important difference of all, but it is also the hardest to describe. It is hard to put into words because the qualities we are referring to are precisely those that painting as a form of art conveys more successfully than language. This emotional quality is defined in the relationship established between the spectator and the objects painted – in the ways in which these paintings go beyond mere picturing of the fruit, to define a position for the spectator. I say 'position', because I mean to refer to a sense of physical placing, as if it were the actual spectator that was the person within touching distance. But it is important to recognize that the painting also defines something more like a *disposition* or inclination on the part of its imaginary spectator. As regards their respective emotional qualities, perhaps the best way to capture the difference between our two paintings is to say that the person we imagine sitting at Moillon's table is a different *kind* of person from the one we imagine sitting at Courbet's. What makes this complicated is that it is the same *actual* spectator – in this case you or I – who is considering both paintings. What we have to say, I think, is that when we experience the Moillon it is *as if* we were one person, complete with one potential range of physical and social and psychological interests and attributes, and when we experience the Courbet it is *as if* we were another. This is to say that each painting solicits a different act of imagination. (I don't at this point want to pin down those differences, because it is important that you explore them for yourself, but we shall return to the question as we proceed.)

If it seems fanciful to think of a painting as working upon the spectator in this way, try to imagine what it must be like for a painter to make such a thing. The artist does not simply measure the emerging appearance of her work against the appearance of the objects she is picturing. At intervals throughout the working process she stands back from the surface in order to test its *effect*. What is at issue is not so much whether the objects look realistic (in the sense of being like their model in the world), but whether the work as a whole *feels* right, or whether its composition produces a sufficiently vivid emotional effect. If it does not, the artist must try to *improve* it. This tells us something about the kind of work that artistic work is. It is work that involves the attempt to make something as good as it can be within its own terms, or to do something as well as it can be done.

There is one case where the work of art needs clearly to match the appearance of its pictured object, and that is the commissioned portrait. But even here it may be hard to distinguish between achieving a likeness and achieving an effect on the viewer – the kind of effect, for instance, that comes from showing a person in a certain light. A skilled portrait painter may create a sense of interaction with the viewer, so that we feel as though the figure were not just seen, but were also *seeing*. (We say, 'It's as though the eyes were following us round the room'.) A portrait may thus appear to be *for* some actual or imaginary viewer. In her portrait by Rembrandt (Plate 9), Agatha Bas seems to look straight out at us, serious and thoughtful. Do you imagine it is you she is looking at? Or do you find yourself looking as if through someone else's eyes? The artist's perhaps? To put the question another way, whose point of view do you think the artist intended his picture to represent? Was it simply his own? Or could he have imagined Agatha to be looking at someone else, her husband for instance? Such an effect might certainly have pleased the husband. In fact Rembrandt did also paint a companion portrait of Agatha's husband, whose name was Nicolaes van Bambeeck (Plate 10). This might appear to support the idea that Agatha's picture was painted *for* Nicolaes – if we assume, for instance, that he would have been the one who paid for both pictures. (The slight difference in the dimensions of the two paintings is due to both having at some point been trimmed slightly at top and sides.) But it's interesting that the woman's portrait is the more detailed, that she's given more prominence, is more brightly lit and is brought closer to the front of the picture. Might Rembrandt have intended to show Agatha as she saw herself, painting her as though studying her reflection in a mirror? It does seem as though he found her the more interesting subject of the two. And we do in fact know that while Nicolaes was a successful cloth-merchant, his origins were relatively humble, while Agatha was the daughter of one of Amsterdam's most prominent citizens, with money of her own. This may not be *why* Rembrandt devoted more attention to the woman's likeness than to the man's, but it does help to explain the *effect* of what we see: the impression that she is posing for no one but herself.

5 TWO STILL LIFES: (2) BIOGRAPHY, INTENTION AND MEANING

We will return to Rembrandt in the last section of this unit. For now, the connection with portrait painting allows us to go one step further in our discussion of the two still lifes (Colour Plates 8 and 9). So far we have discussed them as if all we needed to know could be *seen* in them. But works of art normally come accompanied by other forms of information as well. You may have noticed not only that the two pictures were painted some 250 years apart, but that they were painted by artists of different sexes. It was difficult and unusual for a woman to achieve the status of a professional artist in the seventeenth century, as it was to remain through the twentieth. As a surviving painting by a woman artist of the period, Louise Moillon's work would therefore be exceptional even if it did not have so much else to commend it. Note that she painted her still life when she was only about twenty years old, whereas Gustave Courbet was about fifty-seven when he painted his. Information of this kind may lead us to notice or to look for other forms of difference than those we have explored so far. For instance, we might be inclined to go back to the two paintings and to 'see' a feminine freshness in one and a masculine crabbiness in the other. We need to be careful, however. There is a risk in this case that we will simply reduce the relations between the two paintings to a set of contrasting stereotypes. And these might well turn out to be far less revealing – and of far less relevance to the actual paintings – than the observations we have *already* made without bringing considerations of gender or age to bear.

This is not, of course, to say that either gender or age is irrelevant, nor that when we come to interpret a work of art we can or should set aside such information as we may have gained about it or about the artist who produced it. The point is rather that the *relevance* of such considerations as the age or gender of the artist should be established where appropriate, and not merely assumed at all points. For instance, to accept that difference of gender must be so important as fully to account for the differences between the two paintings would be to rule out or to underestimate the potential importance of the 250-year gap in dates or the 37-year gap in age.

We may, however, be able to use the caption information to confirm our observations and to fill them out. One way to do so would be to recall the point that the artist is always the first spectator of any painting – the spectator, as it were, on whom the effects of the painting are first tried out. Let us say, then, that our first still life is not only a picture of fruit in a basket. It is also a representation of the form and character of Moillon's visual experience. Courbet's painting, by the same token, shows us not only what Courbet once saw; it also reveals, in some measure, the form and character of Courbet's seeing. Now seeing is not simply an automatic process of image-formation. Human spectators are not mere mirrors. We think about what we see as we see it. As we look, our habits and emotions and appetites are in play. The objects of our vision (and of course this includes the paintings we look at as spectators) are continually charged with desire or disappointment, with affection or antipathy – in fact, with forms of meaning. What a man in his fifties desires and dislikes may not be quite what a young woman desires and dislikes. All other factors being equal, we may expect that the pictures they produce will indeed be different, though not necessarily in ways that would allow us to tell which was painted by the man and which by the woman.

Of course, in this case the 'other factors' are considerable. On the one hand, there is the artists' sharing of a convention, a set of implicit rules and expectations, that suggests what is and is not appropriate for a work in the still-life genre. For instance, it was a normal assumption that the appropriate way to paint one's subject was as if it were seen on a table, close to, with clearly illuminated forms against a dark ground. The persistence of this assumption largely explains the similarities we have observed between Courbet's painting and Moillon's. On the other hand, there is the gap in time of some 250 years. This factor may account for all kinds of change and difference. Yet even when these factors are taken into account, what we can perhaps say with the benefit of hindsight is that the *emotional* differences we have found between the two paintings are consistent and compatible with what we now know about the differences between their authors. To that extent each could be said to represent its author. It would perhaps be fanciful to take the next step along this path and to say that each is *like* a form of self-portrait. But to consider the paintings in these terms is not an entirely inappropriate way of drawing attention to their differences, so long as we remember that it is the paintings, not the artists themselves, that we have to test our responses against.

Taking a lead from this idea, we can perhaps use the contrast with Moillon's painting to help us get closer to the 'meaning' of Courbet's. We have considered *what* is represented in the two paintings. We have also considered *how* that representing is done. What remains to ask is: *why* are the objects painted in that particular manner and with those particular qualities? Why such clearly humble objects? Why apples redolent of the country orchard and the long grass rather than the dining table or the sideboard? Why apples that have the signs of decay about them, for all their roundness and colour? Why a single pomegranate? Why a chipped piece of rustic earthenware rather than a more splendid container? And why these forms shown as if glowing with their own light in the near darkness rather than lit solely from above as still-life objects are more normally painted?

The questions perhaps matter more than the answers, for they serve in themselves to indicate what makes Courbet's painting distinctive *as a painting* – an object whose meaning is largely derived from its relationship to other paintings. In fact, to ask such questions is already to show some recognition of what it means to work within a tradition and a genre, for they imply some understanding of the *kinds* of decision it was relevant for the painter to make. If we assume that the properties we have observed are the properties the painting is intended to have, we are really saying that the effect we have experienced *is* the painting's meaning, hard as this effect may be to put into words. But perhaps we can go a little further in explaining why Courbet might have made a painting that looked like this. In order to do so, however, it is necessary now to go beyond what can be learned by looking closely at the painting. There are two points to be made, one relevant to the still-life genre as a whole, the other to Courbet in particular.

Still life, and life and death

The first point, implied earlier, is that the genre of still life has traditionally been associated with a specific kind of moral and philosophical content. If you look at Colour Plates 10 and 11 (Harmen Steenwyck, *Still Life*; Jan Davidsz de Heem, *Still Life*), you may be able to see why.

EXERCISE

Make some brief notes about the differences between the two pictures. List some of the objects in each; then, beside each object, put down a particular meaning or activity or emotion that it suggests to you. (For example, you might write 'peach/eating/physical pleasure'.) The aim of this exercise is not to come up with a complete or correct list – whatever that might look like – but rather to note that the associations of the two pictures tend to go in opposite directions.

DISCUSSION

The Steenwyck features a skull, a large vessel, an empty shell, a watch, a smoking taper, a Japanese sword, a lute placed face down, a book. You may not have been able to recognize all the objects, or to give them all meanings that will fit neatly together. But if you took the skull as your principal cue, you might have deduced that the painting was designed to evoke thoughts of the brevity of life, perhaps also of the transience of sensory experience and of worldly pleasures and achievements. This type of still life is known as a 'Vanitas'. As the full title suggests, the reference is to the vanity – meaning emptiness or futility – of human possessions, powers and pleasures, as expounded in the Book of Ecclesiastes from the

Old Testament: 'Then shall the dust return to the earth as it was; and the spirit shall return unto God who gave it. Vanity of vanities, saith the Preacher; all is vanity.' The second painting, on the other hand, is full of objects suggesting luxury and sensory enjoyment. It seems to convey exactly the opposite message to the Steenwyck: 'Get what you can and enjoy it while it lasts', perhaps. Of course, both paintings were made to be enjoyed as skilful works of art. We might even say that both were also intended to encourage reflection on the brevity of life. But one does so through an encouragement to abstinence and thoughtfulness, the other by a concentration on perishable foodstuffs and momentary pleasures.

It is a feature of the genre of still life, then, that it is often used to suggest deliberation on the meaning and the finiteness of life. This is not really surprising given the two principal conditions that tend to define the genre: on the one hand a type of pictorial set-up that tends to suggest solitary and sedentary concentration; on the other an emphasis upon the play of the senses. In the typical still-life composition of the seventeenth century, the accomplished painter worked to stimulate a sensory self-awareness; the sense of touch is evoked by emphasizing rounded volumes and complex textures; flowers or smoking pipes evoke the sense of smell; succulent fruit, beakers of wine, pearly oysters and the charred flesh of grilled fish evoke the sense of taste; musical instruments the sense of hearing; and of course, the decorative and illusory properties of painting itself provide exercise for the faculty of sight. If you look at Plate 15 you will see a still life by a French artist of the seventeenth century that actually takes the relationship between the five senses (sight, taste, touch, smell and hearing) and the four elements (earth, air, fire and water) as its subject. You may like to work out for yourself which components of the picture are used to represent or to refer to which senses or elements.

Still life and life story

I mentioned two points relevant to Courbet's work. The second concerns the conditions under which he may have painted his still life. He came of peasant stock from the mountainous country of south-eastern France and he retained a strong sense of identification with his background. As a lifelong supporter of political radicalism, he had been involved with the Paris Commune, which was formed in opposition to the right-wing National Assembly in 1871 after the fall of the French monarchy. After the bloody suppression of the Commune, he was tried, fined a large sum for his supposed part in the destruction of the Vendôme column, and imprisoned. (The Vendôme column was a Roman monument erected in Paris, which the Communards viewed as a symbol of oppressive authority and imperialism.) The still life we have been looking at was probably painted in Courbet's cell at St Pélagie prison in Paris.

Given these two resources of information, it is perhaps not so difficult to conceive of Courbet's small still-life painting as a kind of assertion of his identity, and thus by extension, perhaps, as a *form* of self-portrait; not just a picture by, but in a metaphorical sense a picture *of,* someone near the end of his life – a man locked up in an urban cell but with the self-image of an honest countryman, already suffering with the illness of which he was to die, but still, for all that, in full possession of his senses.

There is one important caution to be inserted here. Had you been able to start with the information I have just given you, you might well have arrived at a 'meaning' for the painting by a quicker route than the one I have asked you to take. But you would, I think, have been less likely to do the kind of work the painting invites you to do; less likely, that is to say, to exert yourself fully to *see* it. And it should be borne in mind that the more interesting and potentially relevant the information about Courbet seems, the stronger will be the temptation to use it as a key to the appearance of the painting, *whether it actually fits or not.* If it turned out not to be true that the picture was painted in prison, would this change its 'meaning'? You might feel that it would, and yet nothing would have changed in the painting's *form.* It might be best to say that its meaning *for you* would be affected. But that suggests that its meaning for you is somehow independent of, or separate from, the form of the painting. *If* it is true – as suggested in the block introduction – that a work of art is a 'form given meaning', perhaps it is in the end the form that defines this meaning, and not what anyone happens to feel about it on the basis of the information they are given. It is always tempting to treat biographical information about the artist as a key to the meaning of a work of art, but we need to bear in mind that the formal and physical characteristics of the work are there to be perceived independently of what that information may suggest. The relevance of such information is best treated as an open question. We will turn to discussion of open questions in the section after next.

Before we leave the subject of biography, there is one last point to be made. You may have wondered why I chose to give precedence to Courbet's still life, using Moillon's painting to 'help us get closer' to his, rather than the other way round. The answer is that Courbet is an artist who had a long career, has a substantial body of work attached to his name, and figures largely in the history of nineteenth-century art. I have only ever seen two works by Moillon, of which the still life we have been looking at is one. The other is a painting in the Louvre in Paris, showing a seller of fruit and vegetables with her female customer (Plate 21). Both were painted when Moillon was about twenty.

Though they are both remarkable pictures, there is no large body of later work associated with her name, and I assumed that she died young and that there is little more to be discovered about her. In fact, this was a lazy and unimaginative assumption on my part. It was only at the last stages of preparation of this text that I checked the date of Moillon's death. In fact she lived to be eighty-six. So what happened to her career as a painter? You may have guessed sooner than I did: she got married (to a wood merchant), had children, had another 'occupation'. As a woman married to a successful man, she would not have been expected to pursue an independent profession. When the question comes up, 'Why are there so few great women artists?', it would be worth bearing this lesson in mind.

6 ICONOGRAPHY

I would like to consider one last question about the details of Courbet's painting. What significance should we attach to the single pomegranate in the dish of apples? There is a deceptively easy way to answer this: go to a library and look up *pomegranate* in a dictionary of signs and symbols, and you will find that it had a particular meaning within the classical tradition. Being packed full of seeds, the pomegranate was a symbol of fertility, of life, and of the rebirth of nature. Within the Christian tradition it came subsequently to be regarded as a symbol of resurrection. As such, it may be found juxtaposed with the apple, which stands as a symbol of temptation, of the Fall of Man, and of death. Countless European pictures show Eve tempting Adam with an apple or apple-like fruit, supposedly leading him into sin and bringing about their expulsion from the garden of Eden (see Albrecht Dürer's *Adam and Eve*, Plate 16). In a work of art with a Christian theme, then, a pomegranate may be understood as a symbol serving to remind the viewer of God's forgiveness and of the promise of everlasting life (see Plate 17: Sandro Botticelli, *Madonna and Child with Pomegranate*).

In the traditions of art, it is as if certain forms acquire a life of their own, carrying their little parcel of meanings with them wherever they go. This tendency of pictorial forms to carry and convey symbolic meanings is one of the factors that enables works of art to deal with complex ideas. Where paintings depend heavily upon such symbolic forms of meaning, the viewer may need a specific kind of knowledge in order to 'read' them. The study of such symbolic meanings, of the ways in which they persist and change and develop, is known as iconography. (The term 'icon' is derived from the Greek for an image or likeness.) If we adopt an iconographical approach to Courbet's painting, we may well conclude not only that it is a form of disguised self-portrait or self-assertion, but also that it has a kind of hidden religious theme referring to death and resurrection in explicitly Christian terms.

Once again, you may feel that had I given you this information to start with, you would have been able to 'understand' the painting sooner. But at this point I want to pull back from what begins to look like an exercise in translation (apple = death; pomegranate = resurrection; the beaker full of liquid = communion wine, perhaps). No interpretation of a work of art should be allowed to stand unchallenged if it fails to do justice to the way in which that work appeals to the senses. I am not sure that this kind of translation is useful with Courbet's picture: what holds my attention is the substance and colour and texture of the fruit, and I suspect that it was this sense of substantiality that the painter most wanted to convey. Courbet called himself a 'Realist', meaning that he aimed to show life as it was, not as it was supposed to be. And he never painted a properly religious picture in his life.

The moral is: if pomegranate means – or 'signifies' – resurrection in some paintings, it does not follow that every pomegranate in every painting is there to serve as a symbol of resurrection. It is possible that Courbet had only a few objects available to paint, and one of them happened to be a pomegranate. In the end we can't *know* what the pomegranate 'means', nor even whether Courbet himself was aware of its potential meaning as a symbol for the resurrection. Even if he was *not* aware of it, however, we may nevertheless have to allow that this meaning – having been established in other circumstances – still 'clings' to the fruit.

On the other hand, we should not assume that reading a book of symbols will qualify us to respond imaginatively to the meaning of a given work of art. There are forms of learning that can be distracting if they are not properly harnessed to the exercise of imagination. Given these uncertainties, what we *can* do is to look at the picture – at *all* of the picture – and try to report faithfully what we see, and how we see it. What we can read about Courbet or about Moillon in the history of art may well help us to see and to notice certain aspects of their pictures, and to think to better purpose about how and why these pictures affect us as they do. But what we don't want to do is to let that reading do the work of looking for us. I hope you will have been persuaded by our discussion so far that this work of looking can be both demanding and rewarding.

EXERCISE

This is the moment to look back at your response to the exercise at the beginning of Section 4, where you made notes on the similarities and differences between the two still lifes. There are bound to be points you missed at that stage. Ask yourself what prevented you from making the relevant observations. Try to distinguish between points you might have noticed if you had looked more attentively, and points you missed because you didn't have the necessary information. This may help you to assess your own strengths and weaknesses. You should not feel disappointed on either account, however. It is always easier to concentrate on the task of observation when one has some idea of what to look *for*. ∎

7 OPEN QUESTIONS

AGSG, ch.2, sect.2, 'Your reactions to reading'

The substance of the argument up to this point is that, in order to be in a position to interpret, to explain or to judge a painting, a piece of music, a work of literature or an argument, we need first to consider what its form is. It has to be acknowledged, however, that recognition of a work's form is not *just* a matter of seeing what its components are and how they are arranged. We have seen that there might be doubt about the character of Courbet's still life. Should we see it as a work of straightforward realism or as a kind of 'coded' philosophical-cum-religious statement? In the first case we might assume that the painting of this particular subject is a kind of testimony to the actual presence and reality of these things in the world Courbet inhabited at that moment. In the second case we might regard the components of the composition as having been put together for the sake of their symbolic associations. In asking the question 'How should we see the painting?', we are asking how to discover its *critical* form – the aspect, that is to say, through which significant meaning and value are conveyed.

Here are some other cases in which it can be a complicated matter to decide just what is the critical form of a work.

1   Many works of visual art survive in damaged form or as parts of lost wholes. For instance, many of the early Italian pictures in our national collections are the surviving parts of large composite altarpieces which were broken up long ago. Some of them have been cut down from larger panels. Many are the victims of ham-fisted cleaning or restoration, resulting in simplification of detail and distortion of colour. Plate 18 shows a scene of *The Annunciation* by the Italian Renaissance artist Domenico Veneziano. In fact this was once part of a 'predella' or series of small scenes running along the bottom of a major altarpiece. The altarpiece in question is now in the Uffizi Museum in Florence (Plate 19). At some point, presumably when it was detached from the rest of the altarpiece, the panel was cut down the left-hand side, so that the composition now appears slightly asymmetrical or lop-sided. Can we properly assess the part as a form independent of the now lost or disassembled whole? Would it be better if a section of new painting were added at the left in order to restore the balance of the composition?

2   Does changing the punctuation and spelling of a poem to accord with modern standards alter its form? Or is the poem's form always somehow 'there' in the words, and simply revealed in a different light under different editorial conventions?

3   What do we mean when we talk about the form of a piece of music or a play? Do we mean the composer's written score in the case of the music, and the author's text in the case of the play? Are these the definitive forms of the works in question, independent of any specific

performance? Or in speaking of music and drama respectively, are we talking of arts in which there can be no definitive form *without* performance?

I don't think that these are issues that can be resolved by simple answers of 'yes' or 'no'. Rather, they are open questions. Open questions tend to be questions that are relevant and useful to bear in mind but not necessarily desirable to resolve. They are not always easy to identify as such, and it can be confusing when an open question is presented as if it ought to receive a simple 'yes' or 'no' answer. Imagine that the following question were posed in an examination:

> If you really want to understand the form of Shakespeare's *Hamlet*, should you: (a) study the text in detail, (b) go to one really good performance, or (c) go to as many different performances as possible?

Faced with such a question you might with reason feel under pressure to decide in favour of one alternative over another. But although you might decide on an order of importance, it would not really be appropriate to let any one answer rule out either of the others. To appreciate *why* this is so is to come to some understanding of just what a play is, and of how it is different from more purely 'literary' forms such as the novel and the short story.

Inquiries into form and meaning in the arts often involve open questions such as these. You should not be discouraged by this. It is a part of the enduring fascination of the arts that the problems they pose tend not to have single and exclusive solutions.

8 ADEQUACY AND RELEVANCE

This is *not* the same, however, as saying that any definition of an artistic form will do. Nor does it imply that any one interpretation is as good as another. In the study of works of art there are two requirements to be borne in mind, and in their way they are every bit as stringent as the demands that apply to the study of the sciences.

How much is enough?

I will refer to the first requirement as the demand of adequacy. The experience of the work, that is to say, should be adequate to the work itself. I will explain more fully what I mean by this in the next paragraph. But first I should make clear that to be adequate, an experience of a work of art need not be *total* – as if we could somehow be fully aware of all details simultaneously. Our attention to works of art is necessarily given within certain human limits. It is in the nature of sensory experience that it is subject to a rapid rate of decay. Let us say that someone listens attentively to a piece of orchestral music, such as the Stravinsky extract to which you will be introduced in Unit 3. When it is over, and when experience of its form is thus potentially complete, there will be very few if any people who can at that point bring to mind every note played from first to last by every instrument. Similarly someone might scan carefully over every brushstroke of a painting, or read every word in a novel, but at the point at which they perceive the work as a whole, they are most unlikely to be in a position to recount every detail. In practice one may never 'see' – all at once – all that is there to be seen in the form of the painting, or 'hear' all that is there to be heard in the piece of music, or 'read' all that is there to be read in the work of literature.

The demand of adequacy, therefore, is not that one's looking or listening or reading should always be absolutely complete, but rather that it should be conducted with completeness of experience as its guiding principle or objective. (Of course, in viewing a work in reproduction we are almost always seeing something less than the original has to offer. But *so long as we bear this in mind*, a reproduction can often serve as a reliable indication of the features of the original.) No account of a work of art or of music or of literature can be adequate if the spectator or listener or reader has failed to pay it sufficient attention. So how much is enough? Well, we should not be impressed by someone who offered an interpretation of Courbet's painting which, however neat and tidy, showed no evidence that the glass and the pewter vessel had been noticed at all. This suggests that what is enough is somehow related to what is there to be seen, rather than to the interests of the individual spectator. The measure of what is sufficient attention, then, is not to be decided in terms of anyone's specific priorities, or in terms of the amount of time they have available or happen to think is enough. Rather, the measure of sufficiency and of adequacy is to be derived from the form of the work itself. Though we can rarely give an absolutely complete description of a work of art, we can at least pay it enough attention to understand what such a description would have to cover.

What's relevant?

So much for the demand of adequacy. The second requirement is the demand of relevance. What this means is that we should avoid attributing to the work of art properties that are not actually its own properties. For example, someone might see a painted landscape as cheerful because it happened to resemble an actual place where he once had a good time. But in fact his good time has nothing to do with the appearance of the painting. Similarly, it might be the case that what someone had read about pomegranates, however interesting they found it to be, was in the end irrelevant to Courbet's picture.

Of course, our experience of works of art would be poor indeed if we could not connect them at all with the rest of our lives, with what else we have seen, with what we have read, with our commitments and desires and so forth. But what the demand of relevance means is that we should approach the experience of art as a kind of *responsive* activity, allowing the individual work to guide us in the exercise of our knowledge and imagination, rather than treating it as a peg on which to hang our already formed opinions and associations. It is by observing this demand, I believe, that we come to profit from the individuality or *originality* of works of art – that is, from their *difference* from ourselves and from their newness to us. I have suggested that Moillon's and Courbet's pictures may each be seen as creating its own imaginative world. To see these pictures from the positions they define for us is to enter these different imaginative worlds, and thus to extend our knowledge and experience. This, then, is why it is advisable to leave as much as we can of our baggage of assumptions and interests behind when we engage with the individual work of art. We need to be as open as possible to the promptings of artistic form and composition, for it is through these that we derive the imaginative experience that works of art have to offer. The experience in question is not merely an experience of what is pictured. As we have seen, in the hands of the skilled artist the shapes and colours of which pictures are made can serve to express a range of human identities and emotional dispositions. The perception of independent form can be a *liberating* experience, not unlike the experience of seeing another person as quite different from ourselves, and *enjoying* that experience. It is liberating from self and from those habits of thought and response that serve to restrict the imagination.

With these various points in mind we will now return to the painting by Rembrandt with which we started.

9 COMPOSITION AND THE WORK OF THE SPECTATOR: REMBRANDT'S *THE ARTIST IN HIS STUDIO*

Look now at Colour Plate 1, Rembrandt's painting *The Artist in his Studio*. Note the dimensions. This is a very small painting. The medium is oil paint on a wooden panel. We see a figure of an artist who looks enough like known pictures of Rembrandt in his youth to be reliably taken as a self-portrait. He appears just to have paused in the act of painting. He holds a brush in his right hand, a bunch of brushes, a palette and a mahlstick in his left. (A mahlstick is used when fine control is needed and when it is important to avoid smudging areas of wet paint.

With its padded end resting on the canvas, it provides a supporting bridge for the hand holding the brush.) The artist is well swathed in clothes, as he might have needed to be in an unheated studio in Holland in the seventeenth century. Raised on a log beyond him we see a large and a small stone, used for grinding colours. Two more palettes hang on a nail on the wall. On the table behind him there are bottles that would presumably have held oil and turpentine, both essential in the practice of oil painting. The foreground of the picture is occupied by an easel. The easel supports a thin wooden panel held rigid between two slotted battens. It is presumably from the hidden surface of this panel that the artist has just stepped back.

EXERCISE

Remembering your work in Section 3 of this unit, try to decide at what level the horizon is set and, roughly, where you might locate the vanishing point of the perspective. This should help to establish the angle of the spectator's vision. The clues that may help you to define the angle of vision are the plane of the floor and of the table, and the direction of the figure's gaze. These may also help you to define the perspective, when taken together with the angle of the receding wall and the joins in the floorboards. These last can be assumed to have been parallel in the actual space represented. You will recall that the vanishing point of the perspective is the point where the receding parallel lines would all meet up if they were projected.

DISCUSSION

Given the position from which we see the floor and the table, and the fact that our own gaze seems to be more or less level with the figure's, we tend to assume, I think, that the angle of vision is set at the normal height of a standing figure, and that it is directed towards the gaze of the artist himself. In fact, if I trace the lines of perspective, such as they are, I find them converging on a point to the right of this, in the exact lateral centre of the painting and two-fifths of the way down it, which is thus where the vanishing point is set. We can confirm the level of the horizon by projecting the parallels formed by the battens holding the picture on the easel at top and bottom. Traced out to the right of the picture, these will be found to meet on the same level. The horizon is thus set slightly lower than the level of the painter's eyes. We have already discovered a source of tension within the painting, then. The lines of perspective tend to direct us towards the centre of the composition, while the angle of our vision is pulled inexorably leftwards and upwards towards the figure of the painter, whose eye-level is set slightly above that of the spectator, for all that he seems dwarfed by the easel.

EXERCISE

Now try to draw a ground-plan of the composition – that's to say, a view from above of the area that the picture shows. Mark a line for the 'front' of the picture plane, then draw the room out 'behind' this line, marking the position of the door, the back wall, the easel, the painter and the table. Next mark a point for where you think the spectator is positioned. Bear in mind that although the front of the picture plane coincides with the literal plane of the painting, the spectator's viewpoint may actually be set some distance 'this' side of it. Try to work out an appropriate scale. How tall a man is the artist? How far away is he from the spectator? How far is he from the easel? How large is the painting on the easel?

Next try to work out the source (or sources) of the light. At what height and angle does this light enter the room? Think also about the kind of source it is – a single lamp? direct sunlight? or simply general daylight?

Finally, do you think it is *relevant* to consider what might be shown by the painting on the easel, hidden from us but visible to the painter?

My object in asking you to undertake these tasks and to address these questions is not so that you can measure your conclusions against some set of correct answers, but rather so that you can come to know the painting better. In particular I hope you will gain insight into the kinds of consideration that must have governed its composition and its making. For what you are in a sense doing in considering these questions is addressing some of the same problems the painter must have faced if he was to make this picture out of the material around him.

DISCUSSION

For my version of the ground-plan, look at Figure 1.13 at the end of this section.

If I use my ground-plan to imagine a side-view of the studio, I can begin to work out relative heights for the painter, the spectator and the easel, though I find it difficult to decide just where the spectator should be positioned. To put this another way, I find it difficult to work out the relationship between spectator and artist. We will return to this difficulty, which I take to be significant.

Figure 1.12, then, shows how I think the scene might appear if I were looking in from the side, at the artist's right.

FIGURE 1.12

Now, to consider the light source, we need to look back at the painting itself. The light seems to be diffused and the shadows for the most part soft, as they would be if the room were lit by daylight rather than by a single lamp. The main clues to the direction of the light are the brightly lit corner of the room behind the easel and the shadows cast by the easel, by the painter himself, and by the leg of the table. These all indicate that the light is coming from somewhere relatively high up, almost level with the front of the picture space and to the left of the composition. If I think of my ground-plan as extended leftwards, I can imagine a wall with a high studio window, or a skylight set in the angle between wall and ceiling. There is a lesson to be learned here. The imaginary world that paintings define may be much larger than the space they actually picture.

Finally, we come to the matter of the painting on the easel, and of whether or not it is relevant to wonder what it shows. I think the answer is yes, but only *so long as* this wondering takes place within the 'game' that the actual painting defines – so long, that is to say, as it is a part of our response to what the painting *does* show. To help explain what I mean by this, I will ask you to consider one last question. This is not an easy question, but it is one which I think the painting itself was in some way intended to raise.

Allowing for the effects of perspective, the ratio of horizontal to vertical dimensions is about the same in the picture on the easel as it is in the actual painting we have been considering. What I want to do is explore further the relationship between the two paintings. I offer two possibilities for you to think about.

1   What the painting on the easel would show, if we could only see it, is a picture of what Rembrandt is looking at. He is apparently looking towards the spectator. What this seems to suggest is that the painting is a portrait. If so, it must be a portrait of the one who is both looking and being seen, which is, as it were, you or I. Or rather it is not literally you or I, but a notional seventeenth-century person whose identity we take on in imagination as we become

spectators of the picture. Look again at Rembrandt's portraits of Agatha Bas and Nicolaes van Bambeeck (Plates 9 and 10), and imagine firstly that it is something like one of these that is on the easel, and secondly that what you are seeing in looking at the painting of *The Artist in his Studio* is what she or he would see: that is to say, you are seeing the painter making your own portrait.

2   Of course, the shape of the painting on the easel would be wrong for the typical portrait format adopted for the likenesses of Agatha and Nicolaes. So perhaps what the painting would show is the one we are *already* seeing. Rembrandt is painting a picture of himself in the studio, as if in a mirror. It is his own appearance that he has stepped back to re-examine. It is through *his* eyes that we must imagine ourselves as looking in order to make sense of what we see.

What we have here, I think, is another unresolvable issue – another open question. The tension between the respective possibilities is perhaps represented by the lack of fit between the painting's vanishing point on the one hand, representing as it does the angle of vision of the 'outside' spectator, and the outward gaze of the artist on the other, invoking as it seems to do a matching gaze directed from this side of the picture plane. The critical form of the painting, I think, is the one that serves to keep this tension alive, so that its meaning can never be reduced to a single description.

I chose to concentrate on this painting because I believe it is a work that is concerned with painting itself, and particularly with the relationship between painting and seeing, or between the artist and the spectator. I suspect that the 'hidden' painting on the easel is there to serve in the exploration of this relationship. If so, it is certainly relevant to ask what it shows. What we *imagine* it as showing will only be relevant, however, if it stays within the terms set by Rembrandt's composition.

What Rembrandt seems to be doing is playing upon the different identities of artist and spectator, maker and consumer, rendering them interchangeable. The spectator sees how it is to look *as an artist*. The artist in turn gives an ordering power to the look of the spectator and considers how he himself might be seen by the one whose likeness he is capturing. You may recall a point I made in Section 2 of this unit, about the basic condition for art as a social activity: that it requires both an artist who furnishes materials for the exercise of imagination, and a spectator willing to undertake the relevant imaginative work – or to play the game the painting defines.

There is a way of testing how much of the effect of Rembrandt's picture depends upon the ambiguity of the painting we *can't* see. About a year after he had painted this picture, another artist – who was then one of Rembrandt's pupils and studio assistants – made his own version of the subject, replacing Rembrandt's image with his own (see Gerard Dou's

A Painter in his Studio, Plate 20). The pupil acknowledged his master by the inclusion of his portrait high on the back wall. And he added various still-life objects designed to evoke other kinds of occupation with which the art of painting might be thought to compete: symbols of learning on the shelf at the top and of martial activity in the right foreground. These are the kinds of material that provide fruitful work for the iconographer (a person who studies the meanings of images), and their inclusion in Dou's picture serves to emphasize the complete absence of such devices in Rembrandt's. Gerard Dou was clearly unable to trust as fully as Rembrandt had done to the willing imagination of the spectator.

EXERCISE

Look for yourself at the other changes Dou has made in his interpretation of the theme, and make a brief note of those you consider significant.

DISCUSSION

Two specific changes seem to me of particular significance. The first is the inclusion of a second figure at the far left. This serves not only to signal more clearly the presence of a witness in the studio, but also to give that witness an identity more evidently distinct from the artist's own, presumably that of a patron. The second change, of course, is the turning of the hidden canvas so that its subject is revealed to the spectator. And how banal that subject turns out to be. What a loss the loss of ambiguity is to the *effect* of the composition.

There is an important lesson here, that Dou had evidently not learned from his master. The true complexity and fascination of art – when it is exercised at the highest level at least – lies not in the quantity or lifelikeness of its detail. It lies in the inventive use of its form and composition. It is this that solicits the imaginative collaboration of the spectator.

There is a final question that Rembrandt's painting invites us to consider. How are we to get the most from such paintings, or how are we to equip ourselves to become competent and successful spectators of them? Do we need to learn about conditions in the Low Countries in the seventeenth century, about the organization of Rembrandt's studio, about the social standing and identity of his patrons and so forth, in order to equip ourselves to be imaginative visitors to his studio? In other words, do we need to do some art-historical work and learn how to approach the painting, how to interpret it, how to 'see' it? Or when we talk of the form of the work, are we talking of a form that is sufficient to its own purposes, and that therefore furnishes all the relevant imaginative guidance someone might need in order to 'see' it? If we take the painting on its own terms and adopt the identity it defines for us, do we *become* the imaginative occupants of its world?

There is another way to put this question. Is the meaning of a work of art always relative to what we know about it, or think about it, or believe about it, so that this meaning must always change according to the position from which the work is viewed? Or is what we *mean* by the meaning of the work the identity that it possesses by virtue of its *own* properties, irrespective of our knowledge and interest? In the first case, we might think of works of art as objects that have a kind of continuing and changing life on account of their presence in our thoughts and conversation and writing. In the second case, we might say that although a work might look different to different people, and might be interpreted in different ways according to differences in their knowledge and interests, what we mean by 'the work' is its critical form – the form that establishes value and meaning independent of our interests and that is actually always the same, however hard it may sometimes be to perceive it.

Again, these are not alternatives between which it would be easy to decide once and for all. Among the members of the A103 course team there are certainly some people who lean towards one position and some who lean towards the other. The important point, perhaps, is that each position serves as a kind of check on the extremes of the other. On the one hand, it should be borne in mind that works of art that have remained of interest over a long period of time have usually been subject to a considerable number of 'true' and 'authoritative' and 'irrefutable' interpretations, each of which claims to capture its essential and unchanging quality, but each of which offers a different form of description. On the other hand, to say that a work of art can mean whatever anyone might want it to mean is to accord it no critical independence or integrity – no interesting *difference* from ourselves.

AGSG, ch.2, sect.4, 'Remembering'

CASSETTE 1, SIDE 1, BAND 1

If you have not already done so, listen now to AC1, Band 1, 'Art history' before moving on to Unit 2.

Ground-plan of the composition

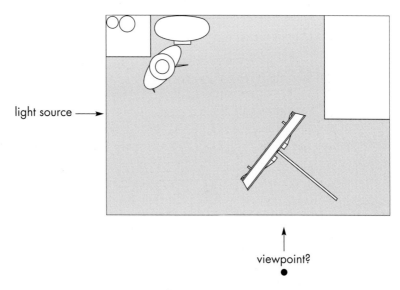

light source ⟶

viewpoint?

FIGURE 1.13   *My version of the ground-plan*

UNIT 2
FORM AND MEANING IN POETRY: THE SONNET

Written for the course team by Stephen Regan

Contents

STUDY WEEK TWO

STUDY COMPONENTS				
Weeks of study	Texts	TV	AC	Set books
1	*Resource Book 1*	TV2	AC1, Bands 2–4	–

Aims and objectives

The aims of this unit are:

1   to encourage you to think critically about the value and importance of poetry in the modern world, both in relation to other art forms and in relation to the culture and society to which it belongs;

2   to interest you in poetry and encourage you to read it (and *hear* it) with sensitivity and involvement;

3   to examine the relationship between form and meaning in poetry, by looking at one particular and distinguished form of poetry – the sonnet;

4   to demonstrate how the sonnet has evolved as part of a tradition of writing and has altered in response to changing historical and political circumstances;

5   to introduce you to aspects of literary criticism and appreciation by giving you an appropriate vocabulary and ample practice in reading and writing about poetry.

By the end of this unit you should be able:

1   to describe some of the basic elements of poetry, such as rhyme and rhythm, and give examples of how they function;

2   to provide a brief account of the formal characteristics of the sonnet and of the range and variety of its subject-matter;

3   to demonstrate how the sonnet form has been modified throughout history, and to suggest how formal innovation might relate to social and cultural factors such as religion, gender and class;

4   to apply some of the basic techniques of literary criticism to specific texts, as a way of appreciating and understanding the language of poetry;

5   to speak persuasively about why poetry matters.

Study note: Bands 2–4

Unit 2 is accompanied by Bands 2–4 of Audio-cassette 1; these bands contain readings (and in some cases discussions) of the sonnets you will be studying in the unit. The sonnets are in the same order on the cassette as they are in the unit: Band 2 contains readings of the first nine sonnets you will study; the next sonnets you study are recorded on Band 3; and the final sonnet in the unit is recorded on Band 4.

The glossary

Words picked out in bold type, for example **rhyme** on the following page, are defined briefly in the glossary at the end of the unit.

Editions and versions

At the end of each sonnet you will find a reference to the source that we have used. However, it may be helpful to know that poems often exist in more than one version, especially where the spelling and punctuation of early poems have been amended by modern editors. Occasionally therefore, in your own reading, you will come across slight variations in the printed forms of these and other sonnets.

1   THE POWER OF POETRY

AGSG, ch.2, sect.3.2, 'Reading speed'

The purpose of this unit is to introduce you to some of the basic methods of reading and interpreting the sonnet. We are concentrating on the sonnet at this point because it is one of the oldest and most popular forms of poetry, and is highly rewarding for both writers and readers. As you will see, part of the challenge for a poet who uses the sonnet is to work within a small space of just fourteen lines. The challenge facing the reader is to understand and appreciate how form and meaning relate to each other. Learning how to read a sonnet is an excellent introduction to reading other forms of poetry. The sonnet is more elaborate than some forms of poetry, but form is essential to *all* poetry, including folk-songs, football chants and nursery rhymes. So the skills you develop in this unit will be useful when you read or hear any form of poetry.

For a discussion on reading a lyric, and writing about it, see AGSG, ch.6, sects 3–6

Most of us can recover from childhood some precious fragments of song or story. 'Looby loo' was (and still is) a personal favourite:

> Here we go looby loo
> here we go looby light
> here we go looby loo
> all on a Saturday night

As a grown-up reader, I can see what charmed the child: I loved those lolloping 'l' sounds and those oodling 'oo's repeated over and over. The quickening pace of 'here we go' builds up and then collapses into a satisfying **rhyme** at the end of 'a Saturday night'. Just four short lines and a couple of rhymes can leave a deep impression. Looby Loo was also the name of a rag doll on the children's television programme, *Andy Pandy*, and perhaps for that reason I began to sing 'here comes Looby Loo'. I must have wanted to give the words some meaning, but first and foremost it was the pleasurable energies of the words that caught my attention. In this way, the form of a poem – its highly organized structure of sounds – can make an impact on its readers and listeners before they have worked out what its words mean.

Some poems seem to function in a way that denies or defies meaning, as if the pleasure afforded by words is an end in itself. Many children's songs take a delight in subverting established meanings, including the Christian message of Christmas carols:

> We three kings all orient are
> one in a taxi one in a car
> one on a scooter blowing his hooter
> smoking a big cigar

oh star of wonder star of bright
sit on a box of dynamite
light the fuse and off we go
all the way to Mexico

(in Paulin, 1990)

Poetry begins with this kind of excited interest in the possibilities of language. Words often acquire a pattern or form in the absence of any plausible meaning, and much of the enjoyment that readers and listeners find in poetry comes from its musical appeal. Poetry, of course, can do many things. It has the power to console, as well as amuse; it can disturb the attitudes and opinions of some readers and transform the hearts and minds of others.

In most cases, though, poetry *does* mean something. One of the basic assumptions in this unit is that form and meaning go hand in hand. We cannot adequately say what a poem *means* without simultaneously recognizing the significance of its *form*. That is why any attempt to summarize or 'paraphrase' a poem rarely does justice to it and can never capture the vivid experience of reading or hearing the poem itself. Poems, like paintings, are imaginative *works*: they involve a process of *making* or *composition*, and the visual arrangement of lines on the page is one of the ways in which the form of poetry can shape the responses of a reader. Like music, poetry appeals to the ear, and the organization of sounds can powerfully affect the way in which meaning is perceived by a listener or reader. What makes poetry distinctive and different from other art forms is its use of words. We can learn a great deal about the way in which poetry works, as both a spoken and a written form, by considering its language as a script for the voice. At a fundamental level, poetry is an *utterance* or *act of speech*, and many of the patterns and structures it uses are those that we encounter in everyday conversation. At the same time, though, most poetry is much more formally organized than speech, through its patterning of sound-effects and its visual presentation upon the page. Briefly, then, we can define poetic *form* as the shape and pattern of words in a poem. The *meaning* of a poem has to do with the emotional and intellectual responses that a poem can draw from a reader or listener. Form is not just a container for meaning; it actively shapes meaning.

Poetry has many forms, ranging from simple repetitive structures such as nursery rhymes to highly organized and intricate structures such as the sonnet. There are many good reasons for starting with the sonnet at this introductory stage. The sonnet is the best known of traditional forms, and there are many celebrated examples that we can turn to for illustration. Much modern poetry looks *formless* or *informal*; learning about poetry at its most formal can help us to understand why more relaxed or irregular forms of poetry nevertheless also shape meaning.

2   THE SONNET FORM

The sonnet originated in Italy in the thirteenth century, and has been used by writers in Britain for nearly five hundred years. Why has it proved so popular? One reason is that, though small in scale, it has immense flexibility: it can accommodate elements of **narrative** or story; it can stage a brief dramatic scene; it can incorporate **dialogue** and imaginary conversation; it can present a series of philosophical reflections; it can explore a vast range of thoughts, experiences and feelings; and it achieves these things within a tightly organized structure of fourteen lines. The sonnet is principally a love poem, but in the course of its development its subject-matter has ranged from the beauties of nature to the horrors of war and from political struggle to religious devotion. In this unit we look at how the sonnet form has been adopted and modified – for significantly different purposes – by a variety of writers working in the English language.

As well as learning to identify the sonnet and understand how it works, you will also discover something of its origins and its historical development. In doing so, you will be looking at a well established *tradition* of writing, with a common set of *conventions* or shared methods and ideas. As you will see, the extent to which a writer can borrow conventions and at the same time modify or alter them is an extremely important issue in the study of literature. The sonnet tradition includes many excellent examples of this process. Each sonnet has its own particular circumstances – biographical, social, political – that influence and inform it. At the same time, each sonnet gathers impetus and influence from a long, evolving history of sonnet-writing, with many prominent and celebrated examples worthy of imitation.

3   SEAMUS HEANEY: 'WHEN ALL THE OTHERS WERE AWAY AT MASS'

CASSETTE 1, SIDE 1, BAND 2

AGSG, ch.3, sect.3.2, 'Broadcasts and cassettes'

Let's begin with a modern sonnet by Seamus Heaney (born 1939), from a book called *The Haw Lantern* (1987). Listen to Heaney reading this poem on the audio-cassette (it is the first sonnet on Side 2), and then listen to it again while reading the printed text opposite. Then try reading it aloud yourself.

FIGURE 2.1   *Seamus Heaney. (Photograph: Caroline Forbes, reproduced by permission of Faber and Faber)*

When all the others were away at Mass

When all the others were away at Mass
I was all hers as we peeled potatoes.
They broke the silence, let fall one by one
Like solder weeping off the soldering iron:
Cold comforts set between us, things to share
Gleaming in a bucket of clean water.
And again let fall. Little pleasant splashes
From each other's work would bring us to our senses.

So while the parish priest at her bedside
Went hammer and tongs at the prayers for the dying
And some were responding and some crying
I remembered her head bent towards my head,
Her breath in mine, our fluent dipping knives –
Never closer the whole rest of our lives.

(Heaney, 1987, p.27)   ■

This sonnet is part of a sequence of eight poems recalling the death of the poet's mother in 1984. The title of the sequence, 'Clearances', suggests 'a clearing away' of many things. At a broad social and historical level, it refers to the clearing of land, including the chopping down of trees, for cultivation. At a more intimate, personal level, it implies a deep loss of family ties and connections. The title recognizes what has been lost, as well as the new space in which the writer must go on living.

The close companionship of mother and son is immediately established in the opening lines of the poem, especially in the phrase 'I was all hers'. A very ordinary and seemingly trivial event – peeling potatoes on a Sunday morning – is endowed with special significance in the poet's memory. The potatoes are 'things to share', and associated with happy sights and sounds: 'Gleaming in a bucket' and 'Little pleasant splashes'. At the same time, they inevitably recall what has been lost, and there are hints of grief, as well as happiness, in the opening lines. The potatoes falling into the water are likened to 'solder', but the word 'weeping' immediately suggests tears, as does the later word 'splashes'.

This is a poem that draws on the rituals of the Catholic Church, as we can see from the reference to Mass in the opening line and, later in the poem, the reference to the parish priest performing the last rites. There's a strange symmetry in the poem between the ritual of potato-peeling, which becomes almost religious or sacramental in its intensity, and the ritual of the prayers for the dying, which takes on the semblance of a domestic task, with the priest going 'hammer and tongs'. In fact, it's precisely this odd relationship between the two events that gives the poem its impulse and meaning. In the moment of his mother's death, the poet recalls that other intimate moment: 'her head bent towards my head,/Her breath in mine.' The poet comes to realize and appreciate the full significance of that moment only when it is too late: 'Never closer the whole rest of our lives.'

So far, we haven't considered the poem as a *sonnet*. But I want to suggest that the poem's power to move us has as much to do with its form or structure as a sonnet, as with its sharing of painful memories. Since its earliest days, the sonnet has been used by poets as a way of expressing love and articulating grief and loss. Let's look at the form of the sonnet and try to understand how it works.

EXERCISE

Count the number of lines in the poem and notice how they are divided.

DISCUSSION

The poem has fourteen lines and each is of roughly the same length. Try counting the separate units of sound or **syllables** in each line, and you will see that most lines have ten syllables. The poem is divided into two parts of unequal length – one of eight lines and one of six. The poem also has a **rhyme scheme**, with line endings creating a particular pattern of sounds. Some words are full rhymes – such as 'dying' and 'crying' or 'knives' and 'lives' – and others are approximate rhymes or half-rhymes, such as 'one' and 'iron'. Play the recording of the poem once again and listen carefully for these rhymes.

What we have described are the basic characteristics of the sonnet form. In Heaney's sonnet, as in most sonnets, there is a strong sense of design or composition which derives from the poem's organization or patterning of words. The sonnet works by structuring and compressing the writer's thoughts and feelings. This is particularly important where deep feelings of grief and loss are concerned: within the form of the sonnet, such feelings find shape and coherence; they are brought into focus.

EXERCISE

I would like you to read Heaney's sonnet once more. Consider whether the poem's structure in some way controls the flow of its feelings.

DISCUSSION

My own view of what happens is that the form of the sonnet compresses the language of the poem and concentrates its thoughts and feelings very powerfully. Poetry might be thought of as language working under stress, and in Heaney's sonnet this *stress* is both structural and emotional: form and feeling are brought into close relationship. As an example of how the form of the sonnet intensifies its emotional impact, I would point out how the division between the two parts of the poem creates a strong sense of contrast, setting a memory of life alongside a memory of death. Also, the closing two lines deepen and concentrate the poem's preoccupation with loss, and this is intensified in the rhyme of 'knives' and 'lives'. The sonnet recognizes and celebrates closeness in the very moment that this is cut irrevocably away, and it leaves us with a sorrowful pang.

---

4 FROM ITALIAN COURT TO IRISH KITCHEN

AGSG, ch.2, sect.4, 'Remembering'

The nineteenth-century poet Dante Gabriel Rossetti described a sonnet as 'a moment's monument', and this is clearly illustrated in Heaney's poem. A deeply felt moment is not only given weight and substance by the form of the sonnet; it also acquires a sense of permanence. This has been a function of the sonnet since it was first used by poets in the thirteenth century. What follows in the next two or three pages is a brief historical account of the origins of the sonnet: this is mainly for reference and you are not expected to memorize it. Although this section may contain some unfamiliar names and terms, it should help you to understand how the sonnet acquired its distinctive character and form. Before reading further about the history of the sonnet, however, you might consider taking a study break.

The Italian sonnet

The sonnet was invented in southern Italy, around 1230, and was probably the work of a small group of poets writing at the court of Emperor Frederick II of Sicily (most of these sonnets are attributed to the emperor's notary and legal assistant, Giacomo da Lentino). So, originally, the language of the sonnet was intimately connected with the power and authority of the court. At the heart of the sonnet form is the idea of *eloquence* – the skilful display of words with admirable wisdom and wit. The name 'sonnet' comes from the Italian *sonetto*, a diminutive version of *suono*, meaning 'sound'. The sound of the human voice, with all its various nuances and inflections, has informed and shaped the sonnet from the outset. Eloquence was an index of power, an opportunity for the courtier to establish a position of status and respect through elaborate and persuasive speech. Characteristic of the sonnet is the assertion of a dramatized self or persona, a speaking voice that appeals to an imagined listener through a carefully staged set of arguments and explanations. The sonnet nearly always involves some progression of ideas and some attempt to reach a satisfying and convincing conclusion.

The perfection of the Italian sonnet is generally associated with the work of Francesco Petrarca, known as Petrarch (1304–74). Petrarch's *Rime* (pronounced 'ree-may') is a collection of 317 sonnets and other poetic forms, such as madrigals and ballads, and it became the most powerful inspiration for the love poetry of Renaissance Europe. By the time Petrarch started writing sonnets in the 1330s, however, the sonnet form was already a century old and highly sophisticated as a poetic instrument of eloquent reasoning and argumentation. What came to be known as the Petrarchan sonnet is essentially two groups making up fourteen lines, with a break known as the *volta* (or **turn** in English) marking the division between the **octave** (a group of eight lines) and the **sestet** (a group of six lines). This turn is an extremely important formal device, since it marks a change of direction in the thought or feeling of the sonnet. It can reverse what has already been said in the octave or it can intensify an existing statement; alternatively, it can move the poem towards a summary or conclusion. (Look back at Heaney's sonnet and you will see that the turn between octave and sestet is clearly marked by the word 'So', suggesting one thing leading to another.)

The rhyme scheme of a Petrarchan sonnet, usually ABBA ABBA in the octave and either CDE CDE or CDC DCD in the sestet, suggests a further division of the octave into two **quatrains** (of four lines each) and the sestet into two **tercets** or triplets (of three lines each). Look closely at the translation of one of Petrarch's sonnets in *Resource Book 1,* A1, and check the rhyme scheme for yourself. A new letter of the alphabet indicates a new rhyme word ('year' = A, 'blest' = B, 'oppress'd' = B, 'prisoner' = A, and so on).

Petrarch is also credited with linking and extending sonnets into a narrative *sonnet sequence,* though this had been anticipated by Dante's *Vita Nuova* (written 1274–91), a sequence of sonnets and other poems with a prose commentary in praise of his beloved Beatrice. (Note that Dante's full name was Dante Alighieri, though he is usually just known as Dante.)

Petrarch's sonnets are addressed to Laura de Sade, who was born in Avignon in the south of France, and died there in April 1348. Petrarch adopts the established convention of an eloquent speaker addressing (as in formal speech) the woman he loves, but he brings to the speaking voice a new and intense desire for beauty, with all the conflicting emotions that accompany the hopes and fears of the lover. After Petrarch, the sonnet came to be regarded as a form with both private and public appeal, both intimately conversational and overtly rhetorical. I don't expect you to remember all the preceding information, but what I *would* like you to remember is the idea that the sonnet *evolves*: the sonnet is adopted and modified by different poets at different times. Although the sonnet is an intricately structured form of poetry, it has great flexibility and versatility. At the outset, the sonnet was principally an aristocratic form; it involved a sophisticated test of skill and intelligence among a narrow social élite. But the sonnet has come a long way from its origins in the Italian court in the Middle Ages. As we have seen with Seamus Heaney, it is equally at home in an Irish kitchen, with the seemingly mundane and humble subject of peeling potatoes.

The sonnet goes abroad

It was not until the 1520s, a century and half after the death of Petrarch, that the sonnet became established in Britain, France and Spain. This revival of interest in the sonnet coincided with a revival of courtly centres in Italy and elsewhere in Europe. The Petrarchan sonnet, with its abiding themes and images of female adoration, became the favourite verse form of courtiers and retained its appeal for well over a century. Petrarch's adoption of the sonnet as a love lyric now fitted congenially into a world of courtly power relations where influential women played decisive roles in the distribution of favours and rewards. The sonnet, then, continued its development within a particular set of social and political relations, even when its ostensible subject-matter was the intimate one of love.

It seems fitting that the first sonnets in English should have been written by Sir Thomas Wyatt (1503?–42) and Henry Howard, Earl of Surrey (1517?–47), at the court of Henry VIII. English courtly society in the sixteenth century bore some striking similarities to that of southern Italy in the thirteenth century, including a preoccupation with graceful conduct and eloquent address. A punctilious concern for decorum produced a courtly discourse brimming with dedications and compliments that sought to please, if not flatter, the listener. You could look, for instance, at Surrey's sonnet titled 'The golden gift that Nature did thee give' (A5 in *Resource Book 1*). The opening hints strongly at patronage in the suggestion that the lady's 'form and favour' can 'fasten friends and feed them'. The sonnet is essentially a plea to an influential woman not to change her mind with 'fancies new'. The speaker pledges his continuing honour and service.

The courtly discourse of such sonnets, then, is intricately tied up with particular patterns of privilege and patronage and their manipulation. Beneath its sweet reasonableness the early English sonnet conceals a deep political insecurity. Wyatt was probably a lover of Anne Boleyn before she became queen in 1533, but was in and out of court favour, and spent several periods in jail. The Earl of Surrey was also imprisoned several times and was eventually beheaded after his arrest for treason.

Thomas Wyatt not only imported the Petrarchan sonnet into Britain but also introduced the first formal changes to the sonnet since its invention. The closing **couplet** that Wyatt devised was a means of displaying courtly wit and wisdom in the manner of a proverb or pithy observation. Wyatt's innovation reorganized the sestet and reinforced its rhymes as follows:

ABBA ABBA CDDC EE

Surrey amended the octave as well, by introducing a greater variety of rhyme words:

ABAB CDCD EFEF GG

(You can see this if you compare the sonnets by Wyatt and Surrey in *Resource Book 1*, A2–A5)

STUDY WEEK TWO: FORM AND MEANING IN POETRY **61**

FIGURE 2.2
Artist unknown, Sir
Philip Sidney, *oil on
canvas, 115 x 82 cm.
(Reproduced by
courtesy of the National
Portrait Gallery,
London)*

CASSETTE 1, SIDE 1, BAND 2

At this point I would like you to listen to Surrey's sonnet, 'Set me
whereas the sun doth parch the green', and briefly compare it with
sonnets by two other notable poets – 'One day I wrote her name upon
the strand', by Edmund Spenser (1552?–99), and 'With how sad steps,

O Moon, thou climb'st the skies' by Sir Philip Sidney (1554–86). All three poems are on the audio-cassette, and together they demonstrate some of the most distinctive features of the early English sonnet.

To begin with, just listen to them: they are meant to be read aloud, and hearing them will acquaint you with some of the special sounds of the sonnet. Then try listening to them with the printed text (in *Resource Book 1*, A4, A7 and A9) in front of you. With each poem, write down the rhyme words at the end of each line, giving each *new* sound a different letter. Look carefully at the pattern of sounds in each case.

DISCUSSION

I hope you agree that hearing a sonnet 'performed' can greatly enhance your appreciation of its form and your understanding of its meaning. Each sonnet has its own distinctive arrangement of sounds and its own particular concerns, but there are several important similarities worth noting. The first point to make is that all three sonnets are love poems: they are all concerned with the constancy of love, even when faced with rejection ('Are beauties there [in the heavens] as proud as here they be?'), impossible challenges ('Set me in earth, in heaven, or yet in hell'), and eventual death ('whenas death shall all the world subdue').

The second point worth emphasizing is that all three sonnets imagine a listener: they imitate actual speech or dialogue and make use of many expressions that we might encounter, even now, in everyday conversation (though other aspects of the language are clearly 'antique').

The third point to stress (one closely related to the preceding point) is that the language of these sonnets is very *dramatic*: the use of questions, commands and assertions creates a lively sense of activity, close to what we might expect from characters on a stage. The sonnet, not surprisingly, has often been likened to a small drama. All of the above points can be amply illustrated in the sonnets of William Shakespeare (1564–1616).

5   WILLIAM SHAKESPEARE: 'SHALL I COMPARE THEE TO A SUMMER'S DAY?'

CASSETTE 1, SIDE 2, BAND 2

We move now to a detailed study of Shakespeare's Sonnet 18, 'Shall I compare thee to a summer's day?' Listen to the sonnet on your cassette recording and then read it in your own time.

Shall I compare thee to a summer's day?

Shall I compare thee to a summer's day? A
Thou art more lovely and more temperate: B
Rough winds do shake the darling buds of May, A
And summer's lease hath all too short a date: B
Sometime too hot the eye of heaven shines, C
And often is his gold complexion dimmed; D
And every fair from fair sometime declines, C
By chance or nature's changing course untrimmed: D
But thy eternal summer shall not fade E
Nor lose possession of that fair thou ow'st; F
Nor shall Death brag thou wander'st in his shade, E
When in eternal lines to time thou grow'st: F
So long as men can breathe or eyes can see, G
So long lives this, and this gives life to thee. G

(Shakespeare: Dodsworth (ed.), 1976, p.20) ■

Before asking how this poem works as a sonnet, let's try to establish some of its basic ideas. To whom do you imagine the poem to be spoken or *addressed*, and what would you say was its main subject or concern? We might assume that the sonnet is addressed to a beautiful woman, but it is now generally accepted that both the speaker and the imagined listener are male. This sonnet is one of a sequence of 154 poems, first published together in 1609. The first 126 sonnets record and celebrate the poet's friendship with a young man, referred to in one sonnet as 'my lovely boy', while the later sonnets reveal the presence of a 'dark lady'. One of the most unusual features of Shakespeare's sonnet sequence is this intense concentration on a friendship between two men. The speaker addresses the young man in Sonnet 18 with passionate and extravagant words. The nature of the friendship between the two men is never explicitly stated, though it is possible that Shakespeare is addressing a patron and using praise and flattery to seal what is essentially an economic relationship.

The suggestion of gay love in Shakespeare's sonnets has been alluded to by later writers, including Oscar Wilde, and there are certainly instances of a more explicit homo-eroticism in the writings of Shakespeare's contemporaries.

CASSETTE 1, SIDE 2, BAND 2

Listen to it again, and try to imagine the poem as an intimate speech. Think about the ways in which the speaker approaches the subject of love. Jot down two sets of words and phrases – those that you think are 'ordinary' or 'everyday', and those that you think are more unusual or puzzling. Use a dictionary if you are in doubt about any meanings.

DISCUSSION

What did you come up with? I expect that you will have found some common expressions such as 'a summer's day', and also some less common terms such as 'the eye of heaven'. The second line of the poem is a good example of this combination of familiar and unfamiliar expressions. How do you think the words 'lovely' and 'temperate' are being used? It seems quite usual to refer to someone as 'lovely', in the sense of kind or beautiful or lovable, but 'temperate' is more puzzling and seems to hint at such things as 'moderate' or 'sober' or 'even-tempered'. We can see, even in the opening two lines of the poem, how Shakespeare starts out with a familiar idea or expression and develops it into something more complex and elaborate. Look, for instance, at the opening reference to summer, and then notice how the idea of summer is developed throughout the poem. There are three direct references to summer – 'summer's day', 'summer's lease' and 'eternal summer'.

EXERCISE

Now read through the poem again, as if you were listening to a persuasive speech, and see if you can relate these three 'summer' references to three main points in the speaker's argument. Write down your ideas before reading mine.

FIGURE 2.3   *John Taylor? (d.1651), William Shakespeare, oil on canvas, 55 x 44 cm. (Reproduced by courtesy of the National Portrait Gallery, London)*

DISCUSSION

My own response would be something like this:

1   The speaker begins by suggesting a comparison between his friend and a summer's day.

2   He then suggests that in some ways his friend is *more* beautiful than summer, because 'summer's lease' (the time allotted to it) is short-lived.

3   In contrast to the season, his friend seems to represent or possess an 'eternal summer'.

Can you see, at this stage, how the repetition of the word 'summer' develops the ideas and arguments of the poem? In what sense do you think the speaker's 'fair' friend possesses an *eternal* summer? One clue to answering that question lies in the use of the word 'eternal' in lines 9 and 12 of the poem. The speaker says that his friend will grow 'to time' (he will reach as far as time can go) in 'eternal lines'. Here, the speaker is using a **pun** or double-meaning, suggesting both 'lines' of descent, from one family to the next, and 'lines' of poetry. In contrast to the brevity of summer, his friend's beauty will be celebrated eternally in the lines of the poem.

Are there any other words that are repeated throughout the poem? What about the word 'fair'? How do you think it is being used here? Line seven of the poem asserts that 'every fair from fair sometime declines', perhaps suggesting that every fair thing (in the sense of every beautiful thing) eventually loses its fairness. The line seems to gain strength from its compression and also from the repeated 'f' sound. Then the word 'fair' reappears, again in a rather odd way, in line 10: 'Nor lose possession of that fair thou ow'st.' Here, 'ow'st' is an abbreviated form of 'ownest'. Summer is 'leased' for a short period of time, but the 'fair' friend of the poet will never lose possession of his beauty, because it will always be celebrated and remembered in the poem itself.

I hope you can see, at this early stage of our reading of Sonnet 18, how even the simple device of *repetition* – repeating 'summer', 'eternal' and 'fair' – can help to shape or develop ideas and arguments. Let's take this point a stage further by thinking about the poem as a form or structure – something that is made or 'constructed' from words.

One of the familiar 'building blocks' of poetry is **imagery**, a set of words that evokes strong sense impressions (usually visual). So, for instance, 'a summer's day' is an image that evokes impressions of sunshine and warmth. The purpose of imagery is to make some vague or abstract idea, such as love, seem more concrete through likening it to something vivid and perceptible. Think, for example, of the famous line from Robert Burns: 'O my luve's like a red, red rose.' The line is striking and memorable because it likens love (and the person who is loved) to a flower, colourful and perfumed. Shakespeare's sonnets make extensive use of particular images; in fact, these images are a major structuring device.

The opening of Sonnet 18 immediately makes a comparison between the poet's friend and the beauty of a summer's day. This technique of presenting one thing as being *similar* to another is known as **simile**. Line 5, however, makes use of **metaphor**, not just *likening* but *substituting* one thing for another, so that the sun becomes 'the eye of heaven'. The metaphor is extended into line 6, where the sun becomes a human face with a 'gold complexion'. The imagery of light is continued in line 8, which refers both to the decline of natural beauty when left uncultivated or 'untrimmed' and also to the guttering light of a candle left 'untrimmed'. It has also been suggested that the line contains a subtle linking of 'nature's changing course' and the 'untrimmed' sails of a boat ('trimming' in all of these instances implying an act of neatness and order). Finally, the words 'fade' and 'shade' also hint at conditions of light (or the loss of light). Imagery, then, can be seen as a way of giving shape and coherence to the form or structure of a poem.

EXERCISE

Imagery is used in many poems and not just in sonnets. We now need to ask what makes Sonnet 18 a sonnet. How would we identify it as such? Here are some brief exercises:

1   Count the number of lines in the poem.

2   Count the number of syllables (the single sounds) in each line.

3   Look carefully at the final word in each line, and note which words rhyme. Label each pair of rhymes with a different letter of the alphabet, starting with 'day' and 'May' as A.

4   See if you can identify a 'turn' – a turning-point in the thoughts and feelings of the poem.

DISCUSSION

There are fourteen rhymed lines in the poem, each consisting of ten syllables. This is the basic form of the sonnet. The poem has a variety of rhymes – seven pairs altogether.

Identifying a turn may at first sight have seemed tricky: Shakespeare's sonnet is printed as an unbroken fourteen-line poem rather than as two sections of eight lines and six lines (compare it with Heaney's sonnet). Even so, we can still observe an octave and a sestet in the poem, with a definite turn between them, introduced by the word 'But'.

Most English sonnets are divided into lines of roughly ten syllables with five stresses – a measure or **metre** known as pentameter. You have seen that Sonnet 18 follows this metre strictly, and the arrangement of its stresses or marks of emphasis can be represented as follows, with accents to indicate the stressed syllables:

Shall Í compáre thee tó a súmmer's dáy?

A line of poetry that repeatedly uses an unstressed syllable followed by a stressed syllable is called an iambic line. Sonnet 18, then, is written in iambic pentameter – lines of ten syllables with five alternating stresses. Iambic pentameter is the most common measure used in English poetry, but you might hear it almost everywhere in everyday English speech, since its rhythm slips easily into those of ordinary conversation:

She líkes a dróp of whísky ín her téa.

Like rhythm, the rhyme scheme in Shakespeare's sonnets is extremely important: it often conditions the way in which we read the poems, and it can shape the meanings we derive from them. Sonnet 18, for instance, can be read not just as an octave and sestet (eight lines followed by six), but as three quatrains (three units of four lines) followed by a closing couplet of two rhymed lines. The rhymed couplet, which Thomas Wyatt brought to the English sonnet, is a very distinctive feature of Shakespeare's sonnets, so strongly marked that it might even be considered an additional turn: it appears to 'clinch' the argument or offer the reader/listener a summarizing statement that has the force and authority of a proverb or **epigram** (a condensed or pointed statement, usually witty or surprising). In TV2, the television programme accompanying this unit, you will see that Tony Harrison likens the structure of the sonnet to that of a joke, with a statement, an elaboration or reversal of that statement, and a punch-line. The basic structure of most Shakespearean sonnets can be represented in this way:

ABAB CDCD EFEF GG

EXERCISE

To test the flexibility of the Shakespearean sonnet form, I would like you to try an interesting exercise. First read Sonnet 18 aloud as a two-part structure, with one statement (in the octave) followed by another (in the sestet). Then read the sonnet again as a four-part structure, with three sections of four lines (each section making its own statement) being followed by a closing couplet. Is there a difference between the two readings? Briefly write down your response before reading on.

DISCUSSION

Taking it as a two-part structure, we might say that this sonnet reflects upon the short span of summer and 'nature's changing course' in the octave and then, in the sestet, upon the capacity of art and poetry to make something 'eternal' by preserving thoughts and images of beauty. This two-part structure is based on contrast – the idea that natural things change and decay as the seasons pass, while a work of art can salvage beauty from the passage of time by suspending it in the imagination of its listeners or viewers.

Alternatively, we might say that the sonnet has a four-part structure:

Within the first quatrain, a question is asked and an answer is provided: 'Shall I compare thee to a summer's day?/Thou art more lovely and more temperate.'

Within the second quatrain, the theme of transient beauty is asserted: 'And every fair from fair sometime declines/By chance or nature's changing course untrimmed.'

Within the third quatrain, the focus shifts to the idea of eternity: 'But thy eternal summer shall not fade/Nor lose possession of that fair thou ow'st.'

And in the closing couplet, the preceding twelve lines are summarized and explained: 'So long as men can breathe or eyes can see,/So long lives this, and this gives life to thee.'

Overriding both the two-part and the four-part structure is a larger, circular pattern. We move from 'thee' in the opening line to 'thee' in the closing line, and from the hesitant question of line 1 to the closing assurance of line 14.

What encourages the suggestion of a very flexible form within the space of fourteen lines is the sentence structure and punctuation of the sonnet. Recent printings of Shakespeare's sonnets have been amended to bring the spelling and punctuation into line with modern styles and expectations. Even so, I think we can see from the punctuation given in the 1609 printing overleaf that a careful reading of the poem requires certain stops and pauses (marked by such things as commas and colons).

EXERCISE

I would like you to read the 1609 version below, noting the early spellings such as 'faire', 'eternall' and (inconsistently) 'sommer', and paying close attention to those moments in the sonnet where a stop or a pause is required. Try reading the sonnet aloud, and then consider the questions printed below.

Shall I compare thee to a summer's day?

Shall I compare thee to a Summers day?
Thou art more lovely and more temperate:
Rough windes do shake the darling buds of Maie,
And Sommers lease hath all too short a date:
Sometime too hot the eye of heaven shines,
And often is his gold complexion dimm'd,
And every faire from faire some-time declines,
By chance, or natures changing course untrim'd:
But thy eternall Sommer shall not fade,
Nor loose possession of that faire thou ow'st,
Nor shall death brag thou wandr'st in his shade,
When in eternall lines to time thou grow'st,
    So long as men can breath or eyes can see,
    So long lives this, and this gives life to thee.

It's fair to say that Sonnet 18 has a lot of stops and pauses, especially at the end of each line; in fact, each line seems to read like a statement in its own right. The pace or rhythm of the sonnet is affected by punctuation, and in Sonnet 18 the punctuation produces a slow and steady movement.

What is it, then – apart from the imagery of the poem – that holds it together and gives it a sense of coherence? Look at how frequently the word 'and' appears, and also look at *where* it appears.

DISCUSSION

What gives Sonnet 18 a sense of coherence and steady progression is its repeated use of joining words or *conjunctions*. You may have noticed that, in the octave, three lines begin with 'And'. In the sestet, which introduces a contrary line of thought, we find a different set of conjunctions – 'But' and 'Nor'. We use these conjunctions in everyday speech, but in poetry we find them being used in a much more strategic or carefully positioned way.

What also gives Sonnet 18 a coherent sense of form and structure is the repetition and parallel arrangement of the phrase 'So long' in the closing couplet. In many editions of Shakespeare's sonnets, the closing lines are indented to emphasize the couplet, and the neatness of the repeated phrase appeals simultaneously to the eye and the ear. The phrase is particularly effective because it carries the double meaning of 'so', suggesting both 'as' and 'therefore'. Each word in the final couplet is a monosyllable (a single sound), which gives a powerful stress to the closing lines, as does the clinching rhyme of 'see' and 'thee'.

The final line has a pause in the middle of the line (known as a **caesura**), which not only produces a pleasing internal reflection – 'lives this'/'this gives life' – but also gives maximum impact to the closing six words. The final line brings into sharp focus the relationship between 'this' (the sonnet as a finished work) and 'thee' (the friend of the poet). The sonnet rests its claim on a belief that each time its words are read or spoken, extended 'life' is given to the friend to whom it is dedicated.

EXERCISE

To end our examination of this sonnet, try now to offer a brief account of the main concerns that it explores.

DISCUSSION

My own response would go something like this: the poem weighs the claims of passing time and nature's change against the promise of a lasting life in the hearts and minds of future generations of listeners and readers (ourselves). The compressed form of the sonnet, including such things as rhyme, repetition and punctuation, embodies in a very powerful way the tension between two sets of ideas – time and eternity, life and death, the beauty of nature and the beauty of art.

AGSG, ch.2, sect.3.5, 'What if you get stuck?'

I'm not suggesting that this is the only way of describing what Sonnet 18 is 'about'. It's very likely that our responses will differ in some important respects! Rather, I'm trying to suggest that the *meaning* of a poem is always something much more than a summary of its themes and concerns. When language is working under pressure, especially in a tightly concentrated form such as the sonnet, the range of possible meanings is rich and diverse. Form intensifies language so that 'meaning' is not easily extracted or paraphrased.

6 JOHN MILTON: 'WHEN I CONSIDER HOW MY LIGHT IS SPENT'

FIGURE 2.4   *Artist unknown, John Milton, c.1629, oil on canvas, 60 x 48 cm. (Reproduced by courtesy of the National Portrait Gallery, London)*

Unlike his contemporaries, John Milton (1608–74) was not a courtier. Indeed he was a strong supporter of the Parliamentarian side in the English Civil War. In his hands, the sonnet form underwent some significant structural changes and became a powerful instrument for comment on public and political affairs. We encounter in his sonnets the steady but impassioned arguments of a puritan republican: we hear not only the voice of a fastidious religious conscience but the voice of political liberty and civic humanism.

It would be wrong, however, to equate Milton's puritanism with the many negative stereotypes of puritanical religion, and to assume he was an advocate of a rigidly severe and joyless existence. Milton's puritanism was a highly principled form of dissent from the corruption and abuse of power in the religious and political institutions of his day. Even in his most intimate sonnets, Milton's non-conformism – his resistance to both the established Church and the established State – beats against the established form of the sonnet and its assumed courtly stance, producing some striking and unexpected effects. The sonnets were written mainly during the years of Milton's political activism and also in the early years of his blindness, roughly between 1640 and 1660. It is one such sonnet that we are going to look at now.

CASSETTE 1, SIDE 2, BAND 2

'When I consider how my light is spent' is a difficult and challenging sonnet. Listen to it on the audio-cassette and then read it several times before attempting the exercise printed underneath the poem:

When I consider how my light is spent

When I consider how my light is spent A
Ere half my days in this dark world and wide, B
And that one Talent which is death to hide B
Lodged with me useless, though my soul more bent A
To serve therewith my Maker, and present A
My true account, lest He returning chide, B
'Doth God exact day-labour, light denied?' B
I fondly ask. But Patience, to prevent A
That murmur, soon replies, 'God doth not need C
Either man's work or his own gifts. Who best D
Bear his mild yoke, they serve him best. His state E
Is kingly: thousands at his bidding speed, C
And post o'er land and ocean without rest: D
They also serve who only stand and wait'. E

(Milton: Main (ed.), 1880, p.75)

To begin with, make the usual notation of its rhyme scheme, and then see if the sonnet falls readily into the traditional octave/sestet division. Alternatively, can the sonnet be read as a series of quatrains, as Shakespeare's sonnet can? Do you notice anything unusual about the arrangement of lines in this sonnet?

DISCUSSION

The rhyme scheme is straightforward. What we have here is the basic Petrarchan model: ABBA ABBA CDE CDE. What seems unusual, though, is that Milton's sonnet provides the turn between octave and sestet earlier than expected. The conjunction 'But', initiating a shift in thought and feeling, appears in the *middle* of line 8.

In addition, the stops or pauses that we expect to coincide with the quatrain endings are frustrated by run-on lines, a technique known as **enjambement**. In lines 4 and 8 the use of a strong pause or caesura, combined with enjambement, prevents us from reading the quatrains as self-contained units of meaning as we did with Shakespeare's sonnet. Similarly, it proves difficult to separate the sestet logically into two tercets, since the subject of line 11 ('His state') hangs at the end of the line and requires the verb in line 12 ('Is kingly') for sense to be made of it. There is, as we will see below, an explanation for Milton's brisk enjambement and frequent transgression of the sonnet's structural boundaries.

His syntax is complicated, and each line seems to depend on the next for some clarification of meaning. Only the final line can be read as a single conceptual unit. Although the closing line is not part of a couplet, it carries the weight and authority of a proverb or maxim (and in fact has passed into the English language as such).

Let's take a closer look at Milton's syntax, since the impression of density and intractability that the sonnet conveys is largely an effect of its sentence structure. You might have noticed that the opening statement, 'When I consider how my light is spent', has no obvious or immediate rejoinder. The structure encourages us to seek some completion of the statement, such as: 'When I do this ... something else happens.' Instead, we have a series of sub-clauses or dependent statements, introduced by conjunctions and connectives – 'Ere' (before), 'in', 'And', 'though', 'and', 'lest' – extending all the way through the octave. The main verb in the octave doesn't occur until line 8: 'I fondly *ask*'. To complete our sense of the opening line, we need to rearrange the word order to give something like this: 'When I consider how my light is spent, I fondly [foolishly/vainly] ask, "Does God expect a full day's work when light is denied [to someone who is blind]?"'

What makes the first few readings of this sonnet seem difficult and confusing is the experience of holding several pieces of information in mind while the main statement remains incomplete. This delaying technique creates suspense, which is highly appropriate since the sonnet's meaning turns on the experience of *waiting*. The convoluted and protracted syntax imitates the speaker's frustrated mental reckoning.

The sestet of the sonnet takes on a more direct and simplified syntax as it approaches its resolution.

Accompanying Milton's suspended syntax we find the occasional use of **ellipsis** or compression, where certain words appear to have been omitted for the purpose of brevity and impact. To grasp the full sense of line 2, for instance, we need to repeat the verb 'spent' from the preceding line so as to give 'Ere half my days [are spent]', taking it to mean 'Before half my life is over'. Similarly, line 4 contains a contraction so that we need mentally to insert 'is', to give 'though my soul [is] more bent/To serve therewith my Maker': the poet's blindness makes him better prepared to meet his God, at any time, and be ready to offer an account of his spiritual life. Milton also makes use of inverted word order, as we see with 'this dark world and wide', where the strategic positioning of the adjective 'wide' after the noun 'world' gives emphasis because of the repeated 'w', reinforcing the idea of unfathomable darkness.

There are two biblical allusions – both drawn from parables in Matthew 25 – which most seventeenth-century readers would have identified and understood. The first is taken from the parable of the wise and foolish virgins, in which the image of a lamp burning is equated with unswerving faith and the need to stand in readiness for the arrival of the Lord. The 'spent' light in line 1 implies a condition of despair as well as physical darkness.

The second reference is to the parable of the talents and the story of the unenterprising servant who fails to invest his talent (or silver coin). Like the servant in the parable, Milton's speaker is cast into darkness. The poem itself functions as a kind of parable in which the poet 'fondly' (foolishly) queries God about his duty. Patience is personified as a voice who 'soon replies' (appropriately, breaking in before the sestet) and calms the speaker's anxieties. Line 10 inverts the expected word order. Although the line surges forward we have to pause to catch the meaning and perhaps reorder it as follows: 'they serve him best who best bear his mild yoke'. Note also that we have to *wait* for the final rhyme 'state'/'wait' to be fulfilled.

Milton's readiness to stand and wait is not an idle condition but a braced attention to the working out of God's will. The ideal of service that Milton envisages is both religious and political, anticipating the establishment of a paradise on earth. In the context of the English Revolution, the reference to God's 'kingly' state is an ironic reminder of that other 'kingly' state – the monarchy of Charles I – that foundered on its own corruption when the king was executed in 1649.

After the death of John Milton in 1674, the sonnet declined in popularity and frequency and did not recover its appeal as a major poetic form for nearly a century and a half. One plausible reason for this is the emergence of the novel as a dominant literary form in the eighteenth century. Readers – who were becoming more numerous with the growth of the middle class – became accustomed to long pieces of writing, whether novels or poems. They developed a taste for epic or narrative verse, especially witty, satirical works such as Alexander Pope's *The Rape of the Lock* (1712). When the sonnet did eventually recapture the hearts and minds of a new generation of poets in the early nineteenth century, it did so with Milton's legacy intact.

For Wordsworth, Shelley and other nineteenth-century poets, the sonnet retained those vital concerns that Milton gave it – the exploration of personal conscience and the declaration of political liberty. Shelley's hatred of political despotism is powerfully conveyed in 'England in 1819' and 'Ozymandias' (*Resource Book 1*, A36 and A37). For Wordsworth, Milton's influence is clear and direct, though his absence is keenly felt:

> Milton! thou shouldst be living at this hour:
> England hath need of thee: she is a fen
> Of stagnant waters...

This particular sonnet carries the title 'London, 1802' and is one of a number of *Miscellaneous Sonnets* that Wordsworth published in 1807 (the full text of this sonnet is in *Resource Book 1*, A32). This was a critical time in which Wordsworth's poetic aspirations were intricately caught up with England's political affairs. In the 1790s Wordsworth was a committed radical who had welcomed the 'blissful dawn' of revolution in France. By 1802, however, he had lost some of that radical enthusiasm and his recognition of England's 'stagnant waters' coincides with his own uncertainty about his role as a poet. He turns from France to England and calls on Milton, England's great political poet, to inspire and guide the nation. Wordsworth's sonnet to Milton views England and English values as susceptible to corruption and decay. Wordsworth asks Milton to 'raise us up' and 'give us manners, virtue, freedom, power'. For Wordsworth, Milton's soul was 'like a Star' and his voice was 'like the sea', but the very act of turning to Milton suggests nostalgia, and much of the language of the sonnet sounds like an imitation of Milton.

7   JOHN CLARE: 'EMMONSAILS HEATH IN WINTER'

FIGURE 2.5   *William Hilton,* John Clare, *1820, oil on canvas, 76 x 64 cm. (Reproduced by courtesy of the National Portrait Gallery, London)*

The task of invigorating the sonnet with the energies of living speech fell to one of the most undeservedly neglected poets in the history of English literature – John Clare (1793–1864). It was common in Clare's time for poets to praise the virtues of a rural, pastoral life in idealistic terms. Not all poets were happy with this approach, however. George Crabbe (1754–1832), for example, wrote dismissively of those poets 'who dream of rural ease,/Whom the smooth stream and smoother sonnet please'. As an agricultural labourer, John Clare knew the realities of the English countryside as well as Crabbe did, and the sonnets he wrote can hardly be described as 'smooth'. At the time Clare was writing, the acts of enclosure were transforming large stretches of common land into private property. This process seriously affected the parish of Helpston where he lived (now north Cambridgeshire) and dramatically altered the landscape Clare knew. Not only did the redefinition of 'property rights' make villagers trespassers on their own land; it profoundly unsettled their sense of security and identity. In Clare's sonnets the relationship between self and nature is a matter of intense and sustained engagement. His deep sense of local attachment is immediately apparent in the earthy vernacular sounds of his poetry: Clare writes for and about a particular place and a particular community.

CASSETTE 1, SIDE 2, BAND 2

Speaking for an alienated social class, Clare sets a new practice in poetic **diction** – one that refuses to conform to the smooth blandishments of Standard English and Received Pronunciation. Listen to the cassette recording of 'Emmonsails Heath in Winter' and then read the poem carefully in your own time, before answering the question printed below.

Emmonsails Heath in Winter

things happening simultaneously in landscape.

I love to see the old heaths withered brake
Mingle its crimpled leaves with furze and ling
While the old heron from the lonely lake
Starts slow and flaps his melancholly wing
And oddling crow in idle motion swing
On the half rotten ash trees topmost twig
Beside whose trunk the gipsey makes his bed
Up flies the bouncing woodcock from the brig
Where a black quagmire quakes beneath the tread
The field fare chatter in the whistling thorn
And for the awe round fields and closen rove
And coy bumbarrels twenty in a drove
Flit down the hedge rows in the frozen plain
And hang on little twigs and start again *Circular*

(Clare: Robinson and Summerfield (eds), 1966, p.195)

How would you describe the kind of vocabulary that Clare uses in his sonnet?

DISCUSSION

The sonnet uses local speech, and this is seen principally in its use of words of a strongly regional or non-standard variety (usually referred to as 'dialect'). We can list some of these words and explain their meanings:

'brake': bracken or fern

'crimpled' hints at both crumpled and crimped (stiffly pleated)

'furze': a spiny evergreen shrub, often called 'gorse'

'ling': heather

'brig': bridge

'awe': an abbreviation for the hawthorn berry

'closen': small enclosures of land

'bumbarrels': long-tailed tits

EXERCISE

Now read the poem again, with a new sense of its vivid, colloquial language. This time, look closely for any other non-standard or 'unconventional' features in the sonnet.

DISCUSSION

One interesting feature of the sonnet is its total lack of punctuation. As well as disregarding minor items of punctuation such as the apostrophe in 'heath's', Clare omits all commas and full stops. In the original manuscript of the poem he indicates the conjunction 'and' with an ampersand (&). Clare's publishers and patrons tried to eliminate his 'radical slang', and 'tidy up' the spelling and punctuation of the poetry in their attempt to sell 'the peasant poet' to a polite readership. The version of 'Emmonsails Heath in Winter' that you have here is based on Clare's manuscript, rather than on the first printed edition of the poem. Clare's seeming vulgarities, however, were not the result of illiteracy but the consequence of his close attachment to a long tradition of oral poetry, including folk-songs and ballads, and a subsequent wariness of print. He weds this oral tradition of song and recitation to the conventional form of the sonnet, and in doing so reinvigorates and perpetuates the sonnet tradition.

EXERCISE

Now read the sonnet again, and try to get a sense of the speaker's relationship with the place he is describing.

DISCUSSION

The sonnet opens with a declaration of personal affection for the heath and the creatures that dwell there, but the sentence structure, with its run-on lines and lack of punctuation, makes it difficult at first to see what connection exists between the speaker and the place. The 'while' in line 3, for instance, seems to link both 'I' and the 'leaves' in the first two lines with 'the old heron': something is happening to both the speaker and the heath *while* the heron is flying. Similarly, line 5 is likely to catch us off balance because of its surprising diction and its unusually compact form. It should read something like, 'And [I also love to see] an odd-looking crow in idle motion swing'. The overall effect, though, is of simultaneous impressions, of an intense and complex relationship between the speaker and the place.

If there *is* a sentence in the opening lines of the sonnet, it doesn't reach a close until the end of line 7 ('the gipsey makes his bed'). There is no sense of division between octave and sestet, though there *is* a kind of turn at the beginning of line 8 (rather than where we would expect it, at the beginning of line 9). The turn is signalled by the abrupt and unexpected 'Up flies the bouncing woodcock', introducing a new series of impressions linked with the repeated conjunction 'And'. There is no concluding commentary or summary at the close of the sonnet; it reaches a close at the end of fourteen lines, but it retains its sense of immediacy with the present-tense words 'start again' (in the sense of 'fly off'). It is as if the speaker's identity has merged with the scene he describes.

The unusual form of Clare's sonnet is nevertheless appropriate to its meaning. It is almost as if the poem wishes to 'keep things going' at a time when such places as Emmonsails Heath are threatened with change. It seems appropriate, too, that this is a *winter* landscape – 'withered', 'crimpled' and 'frozen' – since (despite the lively activity of the scene) the mood seems bleak and melancholic. Clare's attempt to establish his sense of being in relationship to the place he knew at a time of immense social upheaval led to an acute identity crisis. That feeling of alienation worsened as Clare was pulled towards the literary life of London. Later, as an inmate in Northampton General Lunatic Asylum, he produced a desultory but moving sonnet, titled 'I am' (see *Resource Book 1*, A45). The poem speaks of the crushing defeat and loss of freedom that accompanied Clare's deep sense of social alienation.

8 ELIZABETH BARRETT BROWNING AND CHRISTINA ROSSETTI

Before the nineteenth century, the tradition of the sonnet was one in which the man was usually the speaking, acting lover and the woman was usually the silent, passive beloved. In the love sonnets of Petrarch, Dante, Sidney and others, the idealized woman is the object of desire but is not usually seen to have desires of her own. In many instances it is the absence or death of the woman that inspires the poet's love. For a woman to speak openly of her own feelings in a sonnet was very unconventional, even subversive. The sonnets written by Elizabeth Barrett Browning (1806–61) and Christina Rossetti (1830–94) contrast

FIGURE 2.6
*Michele Gordigiani,
Elizabeth Barrett
Browning, 1858, oil on
canvas, 29 x 23 cm.
(Reproduced by
courtesy of the National
Portrait Gallery,
London)*

with a long tradition of love poetry by men, and they simultaneously redefine and reactivate the possibilities of the sonnet form.

Barrett Browning's *Sonnets from the Portuguese*, a sequence of forty-four Petrarchan sonnets published in 1846, stimulated the revival of sonnet-writing in the Victorian period. The title implies that the sonnets are translated from Portuguese. But in fact it was well known, even at the time of their publication, that they alluded to her relationship with the poet Robert Browning.

CASSETTE 1, SIDE 2, BAND 2

Listen to Sonnet 43 and then read it several times, answering the questions printed below:

How do I love thee?

How do I love thee? Let me count the ways. A
I love thee to the depth and breadth and height B
My soul can reach, when feeling out of sight B
For the ends of Being and ideal Grace. A
I love thee to the level of everyday's A
Most quiet need, by sun and candle-light. B
I love thee freely, as men strive for Right; B
I love thee purely, as they turn from Praise. A
I love thee with the passion put to use C
In my old griefs, and with my childhood's faith. D
I love thee with a love I seemed to lose C
With my lost saints, – I love thee with the breath, D
Smiles, tears, of all my life! – and, if God choose, C
I shall but love thee better after death. D

(Barrett Browning: Agajanian, 1985, p.67)

Look carefully at the structure of the sonnet, and make the usual notation of its rhyme scheme. How does the structure of the sonnet contribute to its expression of love? Look, for instance, at how repetition is used.

DISCUSSION

The rhyme scheme is Petrarchan – ABBA ABBA CDC DCD, if we accept that 'breath' and 'death' are near-rhymes with 'faith'. But there is no obvious turn between the octave and the sestet. Instead of proceeding by logical reasoning and argumentation, the sonnet offers a sustained and impassioned declaration of love which runs across all fourteen lines. The poem acquires its emotional intensity from its repeated stress on a single phrase: 'I love thee'. Six lines begin 'I love thee', while another three include the words within their structure. The form is *not* one of simple incantation, however, and there is nothing mechanical in the use of repetition. Instead, the interplay of rhymes and the alternation of end-stopped and run-on lines gives the sonnet a powerful, pulsating energy.

Like Shakespeare's Sonnet 18, this sonnet opens with a question and constructs a set of answers. Likewise, it creates a strong impression of a confiding, familiar voice. The framework of the sonnet might be described as *enumerative*: it actually lists the number of ways (eight altogether) in which the speaker of the sonnet professes her love. Try counting these 'ways' for yourself.

Compared with Shakespeare's sonnet, there is very little imagery and the language seems relatively plain and unadorned. Images of space ('depth and breadth and height'), and of time ('sun and candle-light'), are used very subtly in the octave to intensify the idea of a love that is both spiritual and physical, both yearning for infinity and yet answering each day's earthly needs. This love is given 'freely' and 'purely', instinctively and unselfishly. The sestet proposes an additional four ways of loving – with all the passion spent on past hopes and sorrows; with the intensity of religious devotion; with all the emotions of an entire life; and with eternal togetherness in heaven. The sestet hints at an earlier religious despair in 'a love I seemed to lose/With my lost saints', but the speaker's

FIGURE 2.7
Christina Rossetti, engraving based on a photograph by Elliott and Fry; Graphic, 5 January 1895, vol.51, p.11

new love provides a reason for trusting and hoping in eternal life. It would be wrong to dismiss the poem on these grounds as a characteristic example of Victorian piety. What gives this sonnet its stature and appeal is its confident declaration of a woman's right to speak of love.

Like *Sonnets from the Portuguese*, Christina Rossetti's sonnet sequence *Monna Innominata* challenges convention by introducing a female speaker. The title *Monna Innominata* might be translated as 'the unnamed lady', a reference to the many anonymous heroines in the history of the sonnet. The speaker of the sonnets is one such 'unnamed lady', a female troubadour who addresses an absent man. The sequence consists of fourteen sonnets – a sonnet of sonnets – written between 1866 and 1881. In her preface to *Monna Innominata* Rossetti refers to Petrarch's Laura and Dante's Beatrice as women who have 'come down to us resplendent with charms, but ... scant of attractiveness'.

A more tender portrait might have been created, she suggests, if such women had spoken for themselves. She acknowledges the example of 'the great Poetess of our own day and nation', but suggests that if Barrett Browning had been 'unhappy instead of happy', she might have created a more persuasive female persona, 'worthy to occupy a niche beside Beatrice and Laura'. In *Sonnets from the Portuguese* the speaker finds a way of reconciling earthly and heavenly aspirations, but in *Monna Innominata* the conflict between physical and spiritual love continues unresolved. Even though the speaker in *Monna Innominata* appears to postpone her love on earth for the promise of a greater love in heaven, the sonnets are preoccupied with separation and unfulfilment.

CASSETTE 1, SIDE 2, BAND 2

Now listen to the opening and closing sonnets of *Monna Innominata*, bearing in mind that they are part of a sequence, and follow the discussion on the audio-cassette. You will find these sonnets printed in *Resource Book 1*, A54 and A55. ■

FIGURE 2.8 *Gerard Manley Hopkins, 1874. (Photograph: Photography Collection, Harry Ransom Humanities Research Center, The University of Texas at Austin)*

Some of the most innovative and experimental sonnets in the later nineteenth century were composed by Gerard Manley Hopkins (1844–89), a poet who greatly admired Rossetti's work and learned a great deal from it. You might be surprised, however, to see and hear how strikingly Hopkins's sonnets differ from Rossetti's. (Several of his sonnets are printed in *Resource Book 1*, A59–A62.) I have not set exercises on his sonnets, so it's entirely up to you whether you read them at this point. If you do, you will note that many of the words have accents to indicate which syllables should be stressed. However, you may like at this stage to take a break from reading, and turn instead to the audio-cassette where Hopkins's 'The Windhover' is discussed on Band 3. On this band you will find a range of sonnets by writers who are not discussed in the unit. You may find it interesting now to listen to them and the accompanying discussion. Then continue with the text below, before moving on to your next exercise – the one on Tony Harrison in Section 9.

The many experimental sonnets that Hopkins wrote are evidence of the vitality and popularity of the sonnet form in the late nineteenth century, and these sonnets gave continuing life to the sonnet tradition and promoted further technical innovation throughout the twentieth century. The technical daring of poets such as W.H. Auden and Dylan Thomas owes much to the example of Hopkins – as does the work of Heaney. The resilience and versatility of the form are such that many modern writers have continued to use the sonnet for a vast range of subject-matter. The sonnet could be used in the service of a noble patriotism, typified by Rupert Brooke's 1914 sonnet 'The Soldier' ('If I should die, think only this of me...', *Resource Book 1*, A64), but Wilfred Owen, Charles Sorley, Siegfried Sassoon and Edmund Blunden showed that the sonnet was just as effective in exposing the horrors of war.

The twentieth century has introduced many new voices to the sonnet, and in accommodating these voices the sonnet has ceased to be the preserve of white European writers. The Jamaican poet Claude McKay (1889–1948) wrote many poems in his own Caribbean vernacular, but used standard English with the eloquence of Rupert Brooke when it came to writing sonnets. He emigrated to the USA in 1912 and became a principal figure in the Harlem Renaissance, writing poems that would highlight racial oppression. His sonnet 'If we must die' echoes the opening line of 'The Soldier' (see *Resource Book 1*, A66 and A64), but uses the eloquence of the form as a plea against the lynching of black Americans. Gwendolyn Brooks (1917–), the first black American writer to win the prestigious Pulitzer Prize, has also used the sonnet, like McKay, to write passionately and powerfully about racial conflict. The Caribbean writer Derek Walcott has introduced to the sonnet a range of Caribbean rhythms and cadences, including those of the creole French still spoken in his native Saint Lucia. Walcott's sonnet sequence 'Tales of the Islands' enriches the sonnet tradition linguistically and culturally by showing how the sonnet can be infused with Caribbean sounds and stories. 'Tales of the Islands' presents each sonnet in the sequence as a 'chapter' in Walcott's autobiographical musings on the islands he has left behind.

US women poets have used the sonnet with remarkable flair, the most prolific being Edna St Vincent Millay (see *Resource Book 1*, A67). Sylvia Plath provides a compelling instance of the female writer's relationship with the sonnet. In her early poetry (much of it written while she was in her late teens and early twenties), Plath used the sonnet repeatedly as a way of practising with traditional forms. She brought to the sonnet form a distinctively American subject-matter, evident in 'Mayflower' – one of the sonnets you can hear on Band 3 of AC1:

Mayflower

Throughout black winter the red haws withstood
Assault of snow-flawed winds from the dour skies
And, bright as blood-drops, proved no brave branch dies
If root's firm-fixed and resolution good.
Now, as green sap ascends the steepled wood,
Each hedge with such white bloom astounds our eyes
As sprang from Joseph's rod, and testifies
How best beauty's born of hardihood.

So when staunch island stock chose forfeiture
Of the homeland hearth to plough their pilgrim way
Across Atlantic furrows, dark, unsure—
Remembering the white, triumphant spray
On hawthorn boughs, with goodwill to endure
They named their ship after the flower of May.

(Plath: Hughes (ed.), 1981, p.60)

The poem reflects upon the name of the ship that brought the pilgrim settlers to America. In the white flower of the hawthorn, it finds an appropriate emblem for the blessings that attend the hardships and struggles endured by the pilgrims. Plath uses the sonnet in a careful, traditional way. The division between octave and sestet is clearly marked. (As with Heaney's sonnet, the transition between them is enabled by the word 'So'.) The rhyme scheme is straightforward for the reader (though demanding for a writer), with only two rhyme words in the octave and two in the sestet. It's worth noting that Plath, like Walcott, achieved her maturity as a writer only through a long and sustained apprenticeship to highly structured traditional forms such as the sonnet. In fact, what Plath is working with here is one of the versions of the Petrarchan sonnet that you met in Section 4.

Some of the most impressive developments in the sonnet form in recent times have been made by poets working outside the constraints of Standard English and English culture. Striking innovations have been introduced to the sonnet by Scottish, Welsh and Irish poets working consciously at odds with official 'English' culture. Edwin Morgan's 'Glasgow Sonnets', for example, illustrate very clearly how the sonnet can be adopted within a specific regional or national locale and infused with the cultural and linguistic traits of that place. R.S. Thomas draws powerfully on Welsh history and geography as he contemplates the very act of writing a sonnet in 'Composition' (*Resource Book 1*, A78). The Scottish poet Douglas Dunn has revitalized the form and language of the sonnet, showing at the same time how the sonnet retains its powerful emotional appeal both as a love poem and as a poem of personal loss and sorrow. Sonnets from Dunn's *Elegies* are included in *Resource Book 1* (A81–A83) and in TV2. Wendy Cope (whose work is also featured in the television programme) has shown how the form of the sonnet can be exploited for comic effect.

9 TONY HARRISON: 'MARKED WITH D.'

FIGURE 2.9 *Tony Harrison. (Photograph: Moira Conway, reproduced by permission of Bloodaxe Books)*

We end this unit with a brief appraisal of a sonnet by Tony Harrison. 'Marked with D.' belongs to a sequence titled 'The School of Eloquence', but its main concern is the struggle of the inarticulate – those people, including his own parents, who have been denied the opportunities and accomplishments that come with eloquent speech. The opening sonnet of the sequence is ironically titled 'On not being Milton'.

CASSETTE 1, SIDE 2, BAND 4

Listen to 'Marked with D.' (Band 4 of AC1) and suggest how it differs from other sonnets you have studied.

class

Marked With D. + put in the oven for Daddy + me

When the chilled dough of his flesh went in an oven *A*
not unlike those he fuelled all his life. *B*
I thought of his cataracts ablaze with Heaven *A*
and radiant with the sight of his dead wife, *B*
light streaming from his mouth to shape her name, *C*
'not Florence and not Flo but always Florrie'. *D*
I thought how his cold tongue burst into flame *C*
but only literally, which makes me sorry, *D*
sorry for his sake there's no Heaven to reach. *E*
I get it all from Earth my daily bread *F*
but he hungered for release from mortal speech *E*
that kept him down, the tongue that weighed like lead. *F*

The baker's man that no one will see rise *G*
and England made to feel like some dull oaf *H*
is smoke, enough to sting one person's eyes *G*
and ash (not unlike flour) for one small loaf. *H*

(Harrison, 1981)

DISCUSSION

Harrison's sonnet defies convention by having sixteen rather than fourteen lines, though it makes use of a turn (after twelve lines). It also retains many of the features of the traditional sonnet form, including a regular metrical pattern and rhyme scheme. This experiment had been tried by the Victorian writer George Meredith in his sonnet sequence *Modern Love*, but Harrison uses his sixteen lines with a much greater freedom and flexibility. It might be argued that a sixteen- (rather than fourteen-) line form disqualifies a poem from being considered a sonnet. Harrison, however, is a poet who is thoroughly aware of the conventions of the sonnet and he uses the dynamics of the form (especially its compression and intensity) with powerful effect. As he explains in TV2, he occasionally finds the traditional closing couplet of the sonnet not quite long enough for his needs. In 'Marked with D.' he ends with a closing quatrain. 'Marked with D.' has two groups of twelve and four lines with a turn between, but in other sixteen-line sonnets the pattern can be four quatrains, or three quatrains and two couplets, or eight couplets. 'Marked with D.' has a consistent rhyme scheme, but some lines (such as the opening line) carry additional syllables.

'Marked with D.' is an **elegy** for Harrison's father, a baker, and many of the images in the poem allude to his father's work. The title is taken from a popular nursery rhyme and recalls the practice of marking bread with initials and symbols:

> Pat-a-cake, pat-a-cake, Baker's man,
> Bake me a cake as fast as you can;
> Pat it and prick it, and mark it with B,
> And put it in the Oven for Baby and me.

Interestingly, with Harrison we move full circle from the sonnet back to the nursery rhyme. The point is an important one, because part of Harrison's endeavour is to break the sonnet's long association with class privilege and elevated diction and open it up to the influence of popular, working-class culture. The nursery rhyme about the baker's man hovers alongside Harrison's sonnet. D is for Dad as well as Death, and it also stands for Dunce.

'Marked with D.' cleverly brings together two sets of images, from work and death. The dead father's flesh is 'chilled dough', and his cremation recalls the oven at which he worked; his ashes are like flour ... enough for 'one small loaf'. The steady progression of the sixteen-line form allows the voice of the poem to modulate from sorrow to anger. The repetition of 'sorry' midway through the poem reinforces its concern with language, class and education. Many of the words and images in the poem have to do with a working-class father's 'hunger' for articulate speech and with feelings of inferiority induced by class condescension. 'The baker's man that no one will see rise' combines the earthly and heavenly associations of bread, as does the earlier reference to 'daily bread' (an appropriate allusion to the words of the prayer, 'Our Father'). The line expresses both regret at the father's limited opportunities on earth, and scepticism about eternal life.

In Harrison's hands the flexibility of the sonnet is such that an intimate elegy can shift into an angry condemnation of England and its deeply divisive class society. The sonnet still strives for eloquence, but it is surely a testimony to its resilient and versatile form that it should have started life in the medieval courts of southern Italy and come to be a powerful instrument for the voice of the northern English working class.

In tracing the development of the sonnet as a traditional poetic form, we have looked at only a few prominent examples. Even so, we have seen how complex the sonnet form can be, and we have seen a great deal of variety in the kind of subject-matter the sonnet can accommodate. The purpose of this unit has been to show that literary forms have a distinctive history and tradition: that forms are *made* and *re-made* in different, changing contexts. We cannot confidently and adequately say what a literary work *means* without some knowledge and understanding of how these forms are made and how they function.

GLOSSARY

caesura (pronounced 'si-zéw-ra') strong pause in a line of verse, usually appearing in the middle of a line and marked with a comma, semi-colon or full stop.

couplet pair of rhymed lines, often used as a way of rounding off a sonnet; hence the term 'closing couplet'.

dialogue spoken exchange between characters, usually in drama and fiction (novels and stories), but also in poetry.

diction writer's choice of words. Poetic diction – the kind of language used by a particular poet – might be described, for instance, as formal or informal, elevated or colloquial.

elegy poem of loss, usually mourning the death of a public figure, or someone close to the poet.

ellipsis omission of words from a sentence to achieve brevity and compression.

enjambement (pronounced 'on-jómba-mon') the use of run-on lines in poetry. Instead of stopping or pausing at the end of a line of poetry, we have to carry on reading until we complete the meaning in a later line. The term comes from the French for 'striding' (what we might describe as 'legging it' in English).

epigram witty, condensed expression. The closing couplet in some of Shakespeare's sonnets is often described as an epigram.

imagery special use of language in a way that evokes sense impressions (usually visual). Many poetic images function as mental pictures that give shape and appeal to something otherwise vague and abstract; for example, 'yonder all before us lie/Deserts of vast Eternity'. **Simile** and **metaphor** are two types of imagery.

metaphor image in which one thing is substituted for another, or the quality of one object is identified with another. The sun, for Shakespeare, becomes 'the eye of heaven'.

metre (from the Greek *metron*, 'measure') measurement of a line of poetry, including its length and its number of stresses. There are different metres in poetry. Most sonnets written in English are divided into lines of ten syllables with five stresses – a measure known as pentameter (from the Greek *pente* for 'five'). The sonnet also tends to use a line (known as the iambic line) in which an unstressed syllable is followed by a stressed syllable, as in this line: 'If I should die, think only this of me'. Most sonnets, then, are written in iambic pentameter.

narrative the telling of a series of events (either true or fictitious). The person relating these events is the narrator.

octave group of eight lines of poetry, often forming the first part of a sonnet.

pun double meaning or ambiguity in a word, often employed in a witty way. Puns are often associated with wordplay.

quatrain group of four lines of poetry, usually rhymed.

rhyme echo of a similar sound, usually at the end of a line of poetry. Occasionally, internal rhymes can be found in poetry: 'Sister, my sister, O *fleet sweet* swallow.'

rhyme scheme pattern of rhymes established in a poem. The pattern of rhymes in a quatrain, for instance, might be arranged as ABAB or ABBA.

sestet group of six lines of poetry, often forming the second part of a sonnet.

simile image in which one thing is likened to another. The similarity is usually pointed out with the word 'like' or 'as': 'Like as the waves make towards the pebbled shore,/So do our minutes hasten to their end.'

syllable single unit of sound or pronunciation. 'Sun' is one syllable; 'sunshine' is two.

tercet group of three lines in poetry, sometimes referred to as a triplet.

turn distinctive moment of change in mood or thought or feeling. In the sonnet, the turn usually occurs between the octave and the sestet, though the closing couplet in Shakespeare's sonnets is often thought to constitute a turn.

REFERENCES

AGAJANIAN, S.S. (1985) *'Sonnets from the Portuguese' and the Love Sonnet Tradition*, New York, Philosophical Library.

DODSWORTH, M. (ed.) (1976) *William Shakespeare, the Sonnets and a Lover's Complaint*, London, Everyman.

HARRISON, T. (1981) *Continuous: 50 Sonnets from 'The School of Eloquence'*, London, Rex Collings.

HEANEY, S. (1987) *The Haw Lantern*, London, Faber and Faber.

HUGHES, T. (ed.) (1981) *Sylvia Plath: the collected poems*, New York, Harper and Row.

MAIN, D.M. (ed.) (1880) *A Treasury of English Sonnets*, Manchester, Alexander Ireland.

PAULIN, T. (ed.) (1990) *The Faber Book of Vernacular Verse*, London, Faber and Faber.

ROBINSON, E. and SUMMERFIELD, G. (eds) (1966) *Selected Poems and Prose of John Clare*, Oxford, Oxford University Press.

ACKNOWLEDGEMENTS

Grateful acknowledgement is made to the following for permission to reproduce material in this unit:

Excerpts from 'Clearances' from *The Haw Lantern* by Seamus Heaney; reprinted by permission of Farrar, Straus & Giroux, Inc. and Faber and Faber Ltd.
Plath, S., 'Mayflower' from *The Collected Poems of Sylvia Plath* edited by Ted Hughes; copyright © 1960, 1965, 1971, 1981 by the Estate of Sylvia Plath; editorial material copyright © 1981 by Ted Hughes; reprinted by permission of HarperCollins Publishers, Inc. and Faber and Faber Ltd.
Harrison, T., 1981, 'Marked with D.', *Continuous: 50 sonnets from 'The School of Eloquence'*, by permission of Gordon Dickerson.

UNIT 3
LISTENING TO MUSIC

Written for the course team by Fiona Richards

Contents

STUDY COMPONENTS				
Weeks of study	Texts	TV	AC	Set books
1	*Illustration Book*	TV3	AC2	–

Aims and objectives

The purpose of Study Week 3 is to introduce you to music from different periods and different cultures, and to encourage you to listen to this in a focused way. We will consider the elements of musical language by studying six short pieces in some detail. Each piece has been chosen to illustrate a specific formal issue and to focus your attention on a specific kind of musical 'meaning'.

The skills that you learn from this unit can be used as tools of analysis for other pieces of music, and will be particularly helpful during Weeks 22 and 29. Study Week 3 focuses on the basic elements of music, but also introduces issues such as music in performance, the role of the listener, music as an expressive medium and music in context – issues that will be returned to and developed in Weeks 22 and 29.

How to plan your week

Audio-cassette player

The week's study will involve you in a mixture of activities, but you will always need to have a cassette player to hand so that you can easily replay extracts. Ideally your machine will have a tape-counter: sometimes it will be necessary to rewind the cassette to find particular extracts, especially in the case of Piece 3. If you do have a tape-counter, set it to zero at the beginning of Item 1, and then write down in the unit the number that the counter reaches at the beginning of each subsequent item.

Your study strategy

AGSG, ch.3, sect.3.2, 'Broadcasts and cassettes'

One reason why music can seem difficult to analyse is that we quite often treat it as something that goes on in the background while we're doing other things. However, my advice for this week is that you listen 'actively' to each of the six pieces. If possible, arrange not to be interrupted or distracted by other sounds around you, and don't attempt to do anything else at the same time.

This active listening will help you to do the exercises. For some exercises you will simply be asked to listen to a piece and offer general observations. Other exercises are more detailed and will take you longer, and I have signalled this where necessary. I have also planned the work so that you can take a break at the end of each piece.

AGSG, ch.1, sect.4, 'Getting yourself organized'

When you do an exercise, always try to write down your answers, rather than being tempted simply to think them through in your head without expressing them on paper: putting your observations into words will help to clarify your thoughts. Whenever possible, try to share and discuss your observations with others.

INTRODUCTION

What does music mean to you?

Before we listen to any music, I'd like you to pause and think about what you understand by the word 'music'. Does it mean something specific to you? You might associate music with an activity, such as dancing. You might regard some pieces of music as a challenge to the intellect, while others may convey an almost sensual pleasure. Music can be different things at different times. It is structured sound, but it is also a vehicle of expression, just as a sonnet is both a structure of words and a means of communicating a sentiment. It can be delicious, spine-tingling, soothing, rousing. It can be a skilful manipulation of notes and it can reflect the essence of an era. Just as a waft of a certain scent can evoke a scene, so too can a particular piece of music unlock a memory.

EXERCISE

Below I've given a selection of comments on the phenomenon of music, made by some of the musicians whose work you will encounter in A103. Read the five passages, and briefly list the very different emotions and functions described.

George Martin (referred to in Study Week 29): producer for The Beatles

I am not sure how much cold-blooded analysis has to do with one's passion for a work of art. It is a bit like falling in love. Do we really care if there is the odd wrinkle here or there? The power to move people, to tears or laughter, to violence or sympathy, is the strongest attribute that any art can have. In this respect, music is the prime mover: its call on the emotions is the most direct of all the arts.

(Martin, 1995, p.13)

Judith Weir (TV22): composer

In a way I can think of many uses, but in the end, for me personally, it's just a mode of abstract thought that I enjoy.

(quoted in Ford, 1993, p.113)

Peter Maxwell Davies (Study Week 29): composer

I believe that a composer has a direct responsibility to his community.

(quoted in The Independent Magazine, *3 September 1994, p.38)*

Toru Takemitsu (TV3): composer

The role assumed by composers in modern society ... One view ... is to evoke the human emotions which man [sic] has deep inside him ... and which should not be allowed to lapse into nothingness ... and express these emotions through the intangible medium called music.

(quoted in BBC, 1986, p.7)

Ray Davies (Study Week 29): songwriter and lead singer for The Kinks

Throughout my childhood those songs we sang at family parties reflected our joys and tragedies: our romantic inhibitions unlocked by Mario Lanza singing a popular love ballad, our fears and anxieties calmed by a George Formby ditty; passions were aroused by songs made popular by Bing Crosby and the Andrews Sisters, Vera Lynn spoke for our lost love in 'We'll Meet Again'; Cab Calloway gave my father Fred a chance to step out for an imaginary rendezvous with 'Minnie the Moocher', while Nat King Cole soothed and calmed a troubled heart. Everyone in the family had their own theme song.

(Davies, 1995, pp.38–9)

DISCUSSION

From these five very different statements you learn that – for these musicians – music is both a communal and a personal activity. A composer may be there to serve a community in a practical manner or may feel compelled to write music to unlock feelings. Music may be abstract and intangible (it is, after all, elusive, temporal) but may also excite passions.

PIECE 1
'UM CANTO DE AFOXÉ PARA O BLOCO DO ILÊ' ('ILÊ AIÊ'), BY CAETANO VELOSO

The elements of musical language/Musical cross-currents

Although you might not think that a Beatles song and a Mozart symphony, for example, have much in common, they do use the same basic elements of musical language – **rhythm**, **melody**, **harmony** and so on. This is true of nearly all music, and the differences between pieces of music come from the ways in which the composers treat these elements. So if we know something about these elements, we can begin to see why certain sounds and structures have been chosen, and this makes our listening more interesting and engaging – just as knowing something about the ways in which artists manipulate their raw material, and poets work with words, has already enhanced your understanding of paintings and of poetry. When you listen to a piece of music you will focus, wittingly or unwittingly, on different aspects at different times. By concentrating on these aspects more consciously, you can gain a better understanding of how a piece of music achieves its effects. (Note: as with the previous unit, words picked out in bold type are defined in the glossary.)

Your first piece has been chosen precisely because its main components are clearly differentiated while contributing in a balanced way to the whole. The four main areas of interest are **rhythm**, **pitch**, **timbre** and **texture**, which combine within a musical **structure**. Below are brief definitions of these elements, which will be clarified on the cassette when you listen to the first piece, and to which we shall return during the course of the unit.

All music has *rhythm* of some description – it is possibly the single most important musical element, and refers to the way in which sounds are distributed over time. *Pitch* means the way in which notes appear to be high or low in relation to one another. Composers manipulate pitch and rhythm together to create *melody*, or 'tune', and *harmony* (the combination of notes). Now think back to Unit 1, in which you considered the concept of 'tonal range' in works of art. Artists select colours and shades of colour to produce a specific effect, and the same is true of composers. Like artists, composers have at their disposal a huge variety of musical 'colours' to choose from – a compositional 'palette'. By this I mean the actual instruments for which a composer writes, and the effects produced by these instruments. The technical term for instrumental tone colour is *timbre*. Composers don't just have a choice of instruments at their command, but can also play with timbral variety across the compass, or range, of a single instrument. For example, the highest notes of the clarinet are shrill and piercing, but the same instrument can also produce the most gentle, husky sounds in its lowest **register** (a particular part of an instrument's compass). The word *texture* refers to the way in which lines of music are related vertically and horizontally, how ideas are woven together; the simplest texture of all is a single, unaccompanied melodic line.

All these elements are brought together within a structure. This is the way in which musical events are organized. In the same way that a novel, for example, might present individual characters and then cause them to interact in different combinations, to undergo changes or to experience events, so too might a composer present musical patterns, cause them to interact and to undergo changes. There are a number of traditional musical structures which have been used by composers over many years, as you will discover in Study Week 22. There are parallels to be drawn here with literature: you studied a variety of sonnets, for example, all of which used a basic mould, or structure

CASSETTE 2, SIDE 1, ITEM 1

I'd now like you to listen to the first piece of music. After you've heard it, I'm going to guide you through, referring to the elements described above. The aim is for you to get some idea of what, exactly, these elements of music are, and how they may be used. Now listen to all of Item 1 to acclimatize your ears to the sounds.

DISCUSSION

I hope you felt that there was something in the music that gradually became familiar, perhaps a beat or a swing that you noticed, though the beat itself is quite elusive. It is a very repetitive song, using only a few words and melodic patterns. The words of the song (in Portuguese) are extremely simple:

1 Ilê Aiê – Como você é bonito de se ver

Ilê Aiê – You are so beautiful to behold

2 Ilê Aiê – Que beleza mais bonita de se ter – Ilê Aiê (repeated)

Ilê Aiê – What beauty could be greater than yours? – Ilê Aiê

3 Ilê Aiê – Sua beleza se transforma em você

Ilê Aiê – Your beauty radiates from you

4 Ilê Aiê – Que maneira mais feliz de viver – Ilê Aiê

Ilê Aiê – What a happy way to live – Ilê Aiê

Ilê Aiê – Como você etc. (repeated)

Ilê Aiê – Sua beleza etc.

Ilê Aiê – Como você etc. (repeated)

Ilê Aiê – Sua beleza etc.

Ilê Aiê – Como você ...

CASSETTE 2, SIDE 1, ITEM 2

Now turn to the cassette and listen to Item 2, referring to the words above where indicated. This is an explanation of how the piece can be broken down into its component parts. ■

The cassette discussion focused on the formal elements that make up 'Ilê Aiê'. But there is another aspect of this piece – its 'meaning'. In other words, we are talking about the kind of piece it is and what its function is. While there are many pieces which can clearly be labelled as belonging to a particular genre or type (**opera** is a genre, for example) and emanating from a particular moment in time, sometimes it is difficult to pigeonhole works or to categorize them.

This song is an example of how musical styles may combine to create new hybrid styles. 'Ilê Aiê' is a Brazilian song that draws on popular, urban and folk styles, reflecting the varied cultural influences on Brazilian music – Portuguese rule, the African slave trade and indigenous Indian music-making. It's an example of a song based on the African-Brazilian *afoxê* rhythm, which is a combination of several quite striking, vital patterns, such as the different rhythmic patterns you heard on the hand drums. The rhythm originates in West Africa, and *afoxê* is now particularly popular at carnival time around the city of Salvador in Brazil – as an expression both of an African heritage and of a contemporary style that can involve whole communities of drummers. While it doesn't use the large communities of drummers, 'Ilê Aiê' does recreate the *feel* of the *afoxê*. Another interesting feature of this song is its bright, joyful sound. It was written specifically to express singer Caetano Veloso's pride in his young son, Moreno, whose voice you heard at the ends of some of the lines of the song.

You might like to finish your work on this piece by rewinding the cassette and listening to the whole song again, this time concentrating on the different musical elements and hearing how they interact.

Summary

1   Pieces of music are usually constructed using a number of 'elements' – rhythm, pitch (melody and harmony), timbre and texture.

2   These elements are combined within a structure.

3   Although some pieces of music can be categorized, others defy precise definition because they draw on a range of styles.

PIECE 2
'O PRESUL VERE CIVITATIS',
BY HILDEGARD OF BINGEN

Focusing on a single musical element/Music as a vehicle for worship

Piece 1 contained a number of interacting musical elements. But sometimes composers will choose to work with only one element – or rather to highlight a particular musical aspect, often for a specific reason, as discussed in TV3. Your second piece does just this.

CASSETTE 2, SIDE 1, ITEM 3

Listen to Item 3, which lasts for approximately three minutes. In not more than fifty words, write down what you consider to be the most striking features of this piece.

DISCUSSION

You may have been struck by the very clean, bare sound of the music. This is a piece for a single, unaccompanied voice. The timbre of this voice is strikingly pure and resonant, and the focus is on pure melody, with rhythm assuming a less important role.

We're going to concentrate on the melodic aspects of this piece, with particular reference to the first part of the extract, the first 'versicle'. (The extract is divided into six versicles, which are similar to verses.) The words of the first versicle, in Latin, are shown in Figure 3.1.

Tu mag - na tur - ris an - te al - ta - re sum - mi De - i, et hu - ius

tur - ris cul - men ob - um - bras - ti per fu - mum a - ro - ma - tum.

FIGURE 3.1   *The first versicle of 'O presul vere civitatis' ('O dance-leader of the true city')*

Above each syllable I've inserted a symbol, either a 'blob' or a curved line. A blob indicates that a single note is sung to a single syllable. A curved line, or slur, indicates that a single syllable (for example, 'tur') is spread over more than one note.

CASSETTE 2, SIDE 1, ITEM 4

Listen now to Item 4, the first versicle. Follow Figure 3.1, bearing in mind the fluid feel of the melody. Do this until you feel reasonably familiar with this passage: it may help if you use a pencil to follow the pattern. ■

In its present format Figure 3.1 merely indicates that there is an ebb and flow to the melody: sometimes the word-setting is syllabic (one syllable to one note, as in 'Tu') and sometimes **melismatic** (where a syllable is stretched over more than one note, as in 'mag'). The next stage is to get a better idea of the ways in which the composer manipulates the *direction* of the melody.

CASSETTE 2, SIDE 1, ITEM 4

Figure 3.2 shows the first line of Figure 3.1, but this time the slurs have been drawn to show the approximate shape of the melody. They move up or down, in roughly the same direction as the melody. Listen once more to Item 4, this time following Figure 3.2.

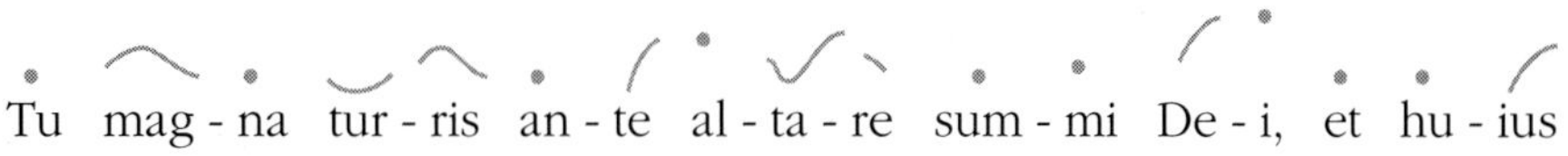

Tu   mag - na   tur - ris   an - te   al - ta - re   sum - mi   De - i,   et   hu - ius

FIGURE 3.2   *The beginning of the first versicle*

DISCUSSION

This time you can see more clearly how the composer moves around her starting point. The gentle, unhurried pitch undulations contribute to the relaxed, serene feel of the melody.

EXERCISE

Figure 3.3 shows the second line of Figure 3.1, but only some of the markings are drawn in. I'd like you to listen again to Item 4, and this time draw in the missing markings – above 'per fumum aromatum' – to show the upward or downward movement. The music moves relatively quickly, so you will probably need to listen to it a few times.

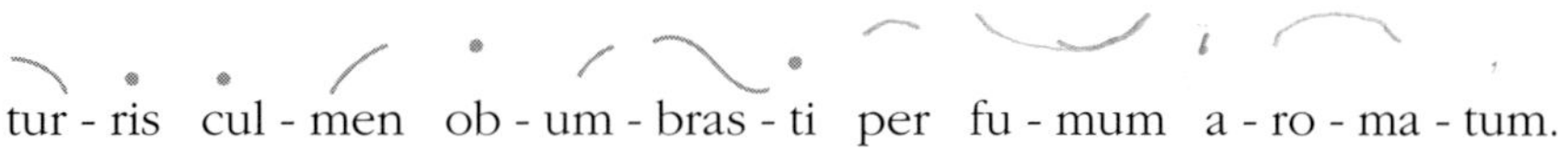

tur - ris   cul - men   ob - um - bras - ti   per   fu - mum   a - ro - ma - tum.

FIGURE 3.3

DISCUSSION

My answer is shown below; as you can see, most of your slurs should have been moving in a downwards direction – but don't worry if your answer does not look exactly like mine.

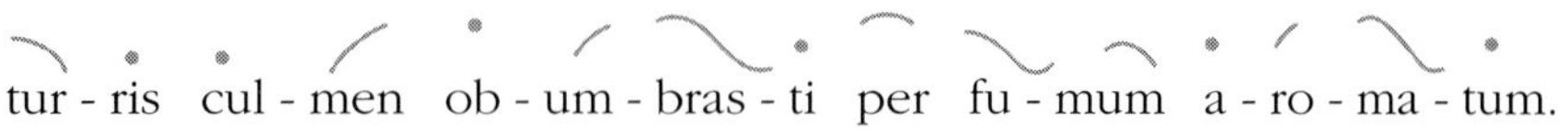

tur - ris   cul - men   ob - um - bras - ti   per   fu - mum   a - ro - ma - tum.

FIGURE 3.4

This system of using dots and slurs is a workable notation system; and in fact, at the time when this piece was written (the middle of the twelfth century), musicians were using a similar system. Figures 3.5 and 3.6 show examples of early notation: the symbols (dots, dashes and curves), showing the general shape of the melody, are called **neumes**.

FIGURE 3.5
Early notation using neumes, showing the melody but not the text (in Grove: Sadie (ed.), 1980, p.353); part of the 'Epifaniam Domino' sequence, Bibliothèque Nationale de France, lat.1118, fol.134 verso

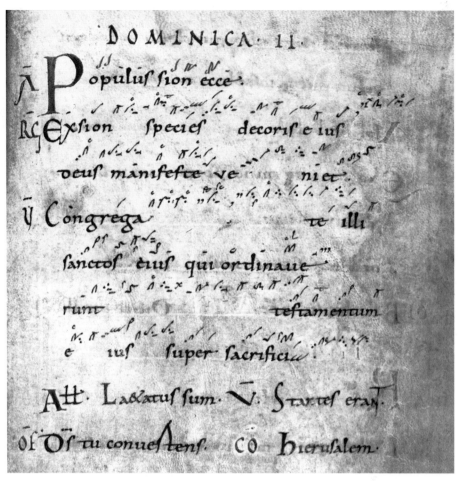

FIGURE 3.6   *Neumatic notation, showing melody and text (in Grove: Sadie (ed.), 1980, p.132); Stiftsbibliothek St Gallen MSS 359, fol.27 recto*

While you have been listening to this piece, you may have started to think about the particular situation in which it would have been performed. Interestingly, the concept of 'performance' as an activity that takes place in front of an audience would not have been applicable to this piece. It was written by Hildegard of Bingen, abbess of a community of nuns attached to the Benedictine monastery of Disibodenberg, near Bingen in Germany.

Hildegard was active as both poet and composer, which perhaps accounts for the very fluid, natural sound of the song that you are studying. Words and music are perfectly united in their reverential purpose. Indeed, Hildegard described herself as being 'a feather on the breath of God'. It was believed that the ideal way of preparing such a piece was for the performer to become immersed in the meaning of the words while in isolation and in a state of reflection. Thus the very simplicity of the music accords with its function: plain, unaccompanied melody is the best way of conveying the devotional meaning of the text.

This particular song, 'O presul vere civitatis', celebrates Saint Disibod, the patron of the Disibodenberg Monastery.

CASSETTE 2, SIDE 1, ITEM 3

The complete text of the song is printed below, both in Latin and in an English version. Read the words carefully and then rewind the cassette to listen to Item 3 (the complete passage) once more. This time, see if you can write down any observations on the overall structure of the piece. The main thing to listen for is repetition of melodic patterns. You've spent some time studying the first versicle, so your starting point should be to see if you can hear the melodic pattern of this versicle repeated anywhere else. Once you have established this, listen out for other repeated patterns. Do use the cassette in the way that suits you: for example, stop it after Versicle 4 and rewind to hear Versicle 3 again, or listen to Versicle 6 and then go back to Versicle 1 to see if there are any similarities; and so on.

Versicle

1 Tu magna turris
ante altare summi Dei,
et huius turris culmen obumbrasti
per fumum aromatum.

You are an immense tower
before the altar of the Highest,
and you cloud the roof of this tower
with the smoke of perfumes.

2 O Disibode, in tuo lumine
per exempla puri soni
membra mirifice laudis edificasti
in duabus partibus
per filium hominis.

O Disibod, by your light
and with models of pure sound
you have wondrously built aisles of praise
with two parts
through the Son of Man.

3 In alto stas
non erubescens ante Deum vivum,
et protegis viridi rore
laudemus Deum ista voce:

You stand on high
not blushing before the living God,
and you protect with a refreshing dew
all those praising God with these words:

4 'O dulcis vita,
et o beata perseverantia
que in hoc beato Disibodo
gloriosum lumen semper edificasti
in celesti Ierusalem.'

'O sweet life,
and O blessed constancy,
which in the celestial Jerusalem
has always built a glorious light
in this blessed Disibod.'

5 Nunc sit laus Deo
in forma pulcre tonsure
viriliter operante.

Now praise be to God
in the worthy form
of the manfully beautiful tonsure.

6 Et superni cives gaudeant
de his qui eos
hoc modo imitantur.

And let the Heavenly citizens rejoice
in those who have imitated them
in this way.

DISCUSSION

Hildegard uses a certain degree of repetition. Versicle 2 uses fundamentally the same music as Versicle 1, with some small changes to take account of the different words. Versicle 3 has new music, this time at a higher pitch, which is repeated in Versicle 4. Versicle 5 has the same music as 6. The overall musical pattern, or structure, is therefore AABBCC. There is also a single note that is central to the piece: every versicle starts on the same note.

You may have begun this section questioning why we were studying a piece of music that consisted of just a single vocal line. What I hope you've discovered is just how much there is to say about something that is very simple – and not only about its form, but also about its meaning.

Summary

1   Sometimes pieces of music highlight a particular element, in this case melody.

2   Music and words can be used together for expressive effect, in this case for devotional purposes.

3   Performing to an audience is not always the essential function of a piece of music.

4   There are different ways of notating musical sounds.

PIECE 3
'INFERNAL DANCE OF KING KASHCHEI', FROM *THE FIREBIRD SUITE*, BY STRAVINSKY

Rhythm and colour/Music for the dance

Your work on Piece 3 will take some time, and you should ideally allow a couple of hours. The contrast between this and the piece you've just heard could not be greater; from a single melodic line to a piece for large orchestral forces – in which not melody but rhythm and timbre are dominant.

CASSETTE 2, SIDE 1, ITEM 5

Listen now to Item 5 complete, trying to focus on rhythm and timbre. If possible, keep a note of the starting-point of this item on the tape-counter, as you will need to find it again later.   ■

For Igor Stravinsky, the composer of this piece, rhythm was the foundation of music, something to be manipulated. Regular patterns were to be contrasted with irregular, sound to be interrupted with silence, and a multitude of different rhythmic patterns to be piled one on top of another. This piece arouses instant attention, with its opening crash and powerful forward momentum.

CASSETTE 2, SIDE 1, ITEM 6

Now play Item 6 for a discussion of some of the interesting rhythmic features of this piece. Figure 3.7 is 'the syncopation diagram' referred to during this cassette discussion.   ■

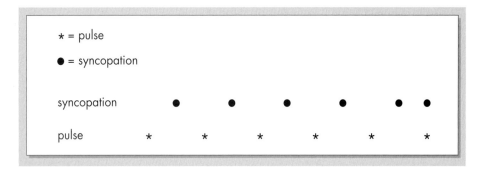

FIGURE 3.7

(Here, as a reminder, are the important points from the audio-cassette discussion. Stravinsky manipulates rhythm in different ways in this piece: he alternates varying **metres**, uses **syncopation** and contrasts rhythmic textures.)

CASSETTE 2, SIDE 1, ITEM 5

Rewind the cassette to find Item 5 and listen to the whole piece again. This time, write down what happens to the **tempo** (speed, or pace) towards the end of the piece.

DISCUSSION

Not only does Stravinsky manipulate rhythm in the ways described on the cassette, but towards the end of the piece he also indicates a gradual increase in speed, followed by a quicker section to close, all adding to the increased excitement in the music.

This is one of the dances from his ballet, *The Firebird*, written for The Ballets Russes – a sensational company founded by the Russian impresario, Sergei Diaghilev (see Figure 3.9 for a drawing of Diaghilev by Stravinsky). The Ballets Russes drew together composers, dancers, choreographers and artists in the first part of the twentieth century, and the collaboration with Stravinsky proved especially fruitful – leading as it did to a whole series of works. The passage below gives the view of British composer Sir Michael Tippett, on the impact and significance of Diaghilev:

> Diaghilev was a unique and quite extraordinary figure. His enormous value, I think, lay in his power to stimulate the general condition of the arts as a whole. He first picked out Stravinsky through his music at a new music concert. He had hoped to become a composer himself. Failing in that, he organized a remarkable Moscow exhibition of new painting. But, naturally enough, he turned eventually and finally to the theatre, where many arts could be combined. And his outstanding and incredible artistic success with his first seasons of Russian ballet in Paris before the First World War, was due not only to the quality of the dancers he assembled, but equally to his inflexible determination to have the same quality in all the arts involved. Diaghilev never made the movements of the dancers an end in themselves. It was not dancing to music; but it was music danced. In the same way the scenery was not just painted wings and backcloths, it was an imagined stage space, wherein the dancers could move, and by which they were also conditioned within the scope of the collaborate enterprise. For what came out of all this was the clear necessity of early conference and collaboration between choreographer, designer and musician ... It was the genius of Diaghilev to bring extraordinary, ever-fresh individual talents into collaboration. The kind of work which resulted was summed up in an aphorism of Cocteau: 'a work of art must be inspired by all nine Muses.'
>
> Stravinsky entered absolutely into this exciting Diaghilevian world. We must always remember that artists like Stravinsky can never be fettered in one art alone, even when the one art is their craft and profession. They inhabit naturally a whole world of sensibility that has as many intellectual and aesthetic forms as there are human tastes and characteristics.
>
> *(Tippett: Bowen (ed.), 1995, pp.48–9)*

The Firebird was in fact one of the first fruits of Stravinsky's collaboration with Diaghilev. It was performed in 1910, though the version that you are studying is slightly later: it was arranged in 1919 into a suite of dances for **orchestra** alone, suitable for performance without the staged ballet. Based on Russian folklore, *The Firebird* tells of a magic bird that rescues the prisoners of the evil King Kashchei. This particular dance is the 'Infernal dance of King Kashchei', hence the decision to use exciting rhythms.

Now that you know a little of the background to the 'Infernal dance', we are going to look more closely at the ways in which Stravinsky works with 'colour' in this piece, in other words with instrumental timbres. Every instrument has its own distinctive timbre that distinguishes it from any other instrument. For this work, Stravinsky chose to use quite a large orchestra, giving him plenty of opportunity to select particular colours for particular effects.

FIGURE 3.8   *Pablo Picasso, Igor Stravinsky, 1917, pencil drawing (in Stravinsky and Craft, 1959); private collection. (Copyright # Succession Picasso, DACS, London, 1997)*

FIGURE 3.9
*Igor Stravinsky,
Sergei Diaghilev,
1921, pencil
drawing (in
Stravinsky and Craft,
1960); private
collection*

Although in one week we don't have space for a detailed study of the
orchestra, it does help to know something about the families of
instruments within it. In fact, the word 'orchestra' does not mean a fixed
number and type of instruments, and the size and content of an orchestra
has changed over a period of some 350 years. However, the backbone
has always been a body of **string** instruments, usually consisting of

violins, violas (slightly larger than violins), cellos and double basses. **Woodwind** instruments, ranging from high to low, include flutes, oboes, clarinets and bassoons. Sometimes relatives such as the piccolo, cor anglais, bass clarinet and contrabassoon are also used. Added to these are **brass** instruments, which may include trumpets, French horns, trombones and a tuba. The **percussion** family consists of a vast selection of instruments that are sounded by being struck. The family has grown throughout this century, particularly with the gradual addition of instruments from non-Western cultures – Chinese temple blocks and Latin American *güiro*, to name but two. You can see most of these instruments in the *Illustration Book*, which contains a photograph of an orchestra (Plate 23).

CASSETTE 2, SIDE 1, ITEM 7

Now fast-forward the cassette to listen to Item 7, which gives three short examples – one of strings, one of woodwind and brass, and one of percussion. ■

Composers use different combinations of these instruments at different times. In the 'Infernal dance', for example, Stravinsky highlights the percussion family by using a wide selection of percussion instruments – timpani (kettle-drums), triangle, bass drum, tambourine, xylophone and cymbals.

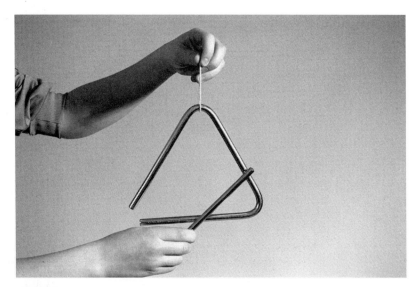

FIGURE 3.10
Some of the percussion instruments used in the 'Infernal dance'. Top: triangle; middle: tambourine; bottom: cymbal. (Instruments photographed courtesy of the Music Centre, Stantonbury Campus, Milton Keynes. Photograph: Mike Levers/The Open University)

CASSETTE 2, SIDE 1, ITEM 8

In the illustrated discussion on Item 8, you can hear more clearly what Stravinsky achieves in the way of instrumental colour or timbre using some of the percussion, brass, string and woodwind instruments. Listen now to this item, which lasts for about thirteen minutes. ■

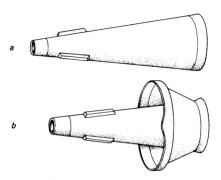

FIGURE 3.11   *Two of the trumpet mutes discussed in Item 8; a = 'straight' mute, b = cup mute (in Baines (ed.), 1992, p.217). (Reproduced by permission of Oxford University Press)*

Here, as a reminder, are five key points from the audio-cassette discussion:

(a) Percussion instruments may be of definite pitch (as in the case of the timpani, for example) or indefinite pitch (for example, the triangle).

(b) Timpani are tuned to different pitches and are played with sticks made of a variety of materials.

(c) Brass instruments can be used to provide special effects, such as a **glissando**; sometimes a **mute** is used.

(d) Stravinsky asks the string-players to play both **pizzicato** and with the bow, and to use **double-stopping**.

(e) Stravinsky uses the full range of notes on the woodwind instruments.

The cassette discussion in Item 8 demonstrated some of the individual instrumental parts that go to make up this piece. As well as using a large orchestra, Stravinsky exploits the ranges of the instruments and the effects that he can achieve from them. You've heard a selection of instruments playing their separate parts, but of course in combination there is still more that Stravinsky can accomplish, choosing certain combinations for specific timbral effects. The piece opens with low instruments: in addition to the timpani, there are bassoons, French horns and double bass. There are also completely different passages where the brilliant timbres of flute and trumpet are exploited. A full orchestra will produce a bigger noise than a single instrument, but an individual instrument can also produce both quiet and loud sounds. **Dynamics** are instructions to the performer to play at a certain volume, and Stravinsky uses a wide range of dynamics in this piece. Short, brittle sounds are contrasted with smooth ones until all the instruments of the orchestra come together for a dazzling concluding section.

Finish your work on Piece 3 by rewinding the tape once more to listen to Item 5 complete. This time you should be able to hear more of the instrumental effects discussed – in particular loud, powerful brass, scurrying woodwind over string tunes, and pizzicato strings. ■

Summary

1   Composers work with rhythm in different ways: for example, establishing and changing metres, and using contrasting rhythmic patterns.

2   Composers use timbre to suit a particular purpose, in this case to contribute to a colourful, evocative dance.

3   There are different ways of producing sound on an instrument.

PIECE 4
'DOVE SONO', FROM *THE MARRIAGE OF FIGARO*, BY MOZART

Melody and meaning

Melody can be used in many ways: Piece 1 had a repetitive, catchy tune, and Piece 2 was an example of simple, undulating melody used for religious expression. Piece 4, where melody is used to convey changing emotions, has been chosen for its extraordinarily expressive qualities.

Piece 4 is recorded as Item 9 on your cassette; the words of Item 9 are shown below. Before you listen to the music, read through the words in their English version (unless you read Italian) and write down what you understand to be the most important feelings expressed. Then listen to the whole piece, while looking at the words, and jot down some of the ways in which the feelings in the words are expressed through the music. Note that you will hear Item 9 sung in Italian and that some of the words below are repeated: after singing the first eight lines, with some repetitions, the singer goes back to the beginning, repeats the first four lines only, and then jumps from '...menzogner?' to 'Ah, se almen...'. At this stage don't try to give a detailed answer to my question, but listen only for the main, most obvious ways in which the music matches the words.

Dove sono i bei momenti	*Where are the beautiful bygone moments*
Di dolcezza, e di piacer,	*Of enjoyment and of content?*
Dove andaro i giuramenti	*Where have vanished the vows and*
Di quel labbro menzogner?	*sighings*
Perchè mai, se in pianti e in	*Of those lips proved so untrue?*
pene	*Why then now if into tears and into sorrow*
Per me tutto si cangiò,	*For me all has been so changed,*
La memoria di quel bene	*Has remembrance of that sweetness*
Dal mio sen non trapassò?	*From my breast not been erased?*
Ah, se almen la mia costanza	*Ah, if only my longing devotion*
Nel languire amando ognor,	*In despair still strong as before,*
Mi portasse una speranza	*Might bring me some expectation*
Di cangiar l'ingrato cor!	*Of changing that faithless heart.*

DISCUSSION

From a first listening, you may have noticed some of the following points:

Just as the words are separated into two parts, so the piece is divided into two types of music. The first part is slower and more poignant, the singer disclosing the anguish caused to her by her husband's infidelity. The second part is more forceful: the singer's hope inspires faster, more spirited music.

This is an extract from an opera, written in the **Classical** period. More specifically, it is an **aria** – a song sung at a moment when the action on stage pauses to allow a soloist, one of the characters in the opera, to reflect on a situation and to convey a particular emotion.

We're now going to examine the piece more thoroughly, looking at some of the detailed ways in which Mozart structures the aria.

CASSETTE 2, SIDE 2, ITEM 10

Aria: first part

Listen to this first, slower part of the aria, Item 10 on the cassette, and answer two questions:

1   In general terms, what sort of role does the orchestra play?

2   When the singer returns to the words 'Dove sono', what happens to the music?

(Item 10 is the first item on Side 2.)

DISCUSSION

1   Mozart uses a relatively small orchestra. In order to clarify this, compare this orchestra with the orchestra in the Stravinsky extract that you've just heard. Stravinsky had many more instruments at his disposal and treated them in an adventurous manner. Here Mozart uses only strings, a few woodwind and brass instruments and no percussion. Because the focus is on the voice, the orchestra has a less prominent role. For most of the time it provides a simple **accompaniment**, though you may have noticed that when the voice reaches the words 'Perchè mai', the orchestra has more to do.

2   When the singer returns to the words 'Dove sono', the music from the first 'Dove sono' is repeated, but the ending is slightly different. Composers often work with compositional formulae, and the first part of Mozart's aria uses one of these. Mozart presents a theme (A), contrasts it with a different theme (B), and then returns to the original theme (A). This was, and indeed still is, a commonly used musical structure.

CASSETTE 2, SIDE 2, ITEM 10

Now we will turn to Figure 3.12 and the questions it contains. Listen again to the first part of the aria (Item 10), as often as you like, answering the questions in Figure 3.12. (Feel free to write in the unit itself.) This is a long exercise, and you are certainly not expected to be able to answer all these questions straight away. My advice is to spend at least one playing simply following Figure 3.12 without attempting to answer the questions, and then spend several more playings answering the questions.

Dove sono i bei momenti di dolcezza, e di piacer,

Which instruments play
at the very opening, with
the singer's first word?

strings

A solo instrument is heard as the singer pauses
after the word *piacer*. Is this a woodwind or
a brass instrument?

*flute × woodwind —
oboe*

Dove andaro i giuramenti di quel labbro menzogner, di quel labbro menzogner? *

In which direction is the
voice-line moving at this
point? Why?
(Look at the meaning
of the words.)

lands + high

Perchè mai, se in pianti e in pene per me tutto si cangiò, per me tutto si cangiò,

During this section, how do voice and orchestra interweave? And how does the mood change?

*on long sung notes orchestra plays tune
+ join in together sometimes*

q + a effect.

La memoria di quel bene dal mio sen non trapassò, la memoria di quel ben non trapassò?

Dove sono i bei momenti di dolcezza, e di piacer,

Dove andaro i giuramenti di quel labbro menzogner?

lands + higher here

quieter, slow + lower 1st time

Compare the ending here with the
ending at * above. How does it differ?

FIGURE 3.12 'Dove sono', first part

DISCUSSION

That exercise was intended to give you a better idea of what is happening musically in this part of the aria. Answers to the questions are as follows:

1   *Which instruments play at the very opening, with the singer's first word?*

Only strings play at the very opening; the woodwind instruments do not enter until the final syllable of the word *sono*.

2   *A solo instrument is heard as the singer pauses after the word 'piacer'. Is this a woodwind or a brass instrument?*

It is woodwind: the oboe provides a decorative, falling interjection at this point.

3   *In which direction is the voice-line moving at this point? Why?*

The voice uses progressively higher pitches. The increased drama of the words ('lips proved so untrue') may well be the reason why Mozart gives the voice a correspondingly dramatic line.

4   *During this section, how do voice and orchestra interweave? And how does the mood change?*

The orchestra is generally more important here, with greater movement and more complex part-writing. There is a 'question and answer' effect between the voice and the orchestra, and in particular between the voice and the woodwind section. The mood is more plaintive to match the words 'tears' and 'sorrow', with a greater sense of drama at 'for me all has been so changed'.

5   *Compare the ending here with the ending at * above. How does it differ?*

This time the singer sings the words *di quel labbro menzogner?* only once; and, instead of ending in a way that sounds complete, the passage ends with a feeling of anticipation, with the singer holding the note in preparation for the faster music to come.

You already know that this is an aria from an opera and that it is an expression of anguish. This is the time to tell you more. The singer is the Countess Almaviva, betrayed by her husband who had once wooed and loved only her. The aria is her opportunity to express her grief, and Mozart uses the formal elements of music to achieve this. From the work that you have already completed, you can draw some conclusions about the ways in which he goes about this. As regards timbre, you know that he uses a small orchestra, but increases its prominence at crucial moments for specific effects. And you know that the pitch of the singer's line sometimes rises in accordance with the growing tensions of the words. But we have not yet discussed the main way in which poignancy is achieved, and this is through Mozart's use of melody. The emphasis on balanced, yearning melody is what makes this so effective. One of the ways in which Mozart achieves the 'yearning' element is by leaning on or emphasizing certain notes, usually at the end of a **phrase** (a short, distinct piece of melody).

CASSETTE 2, SIDE 2, ITEM 10

Listen once more to Item 10, this time concentrating on these leaning effects and on the way in which the underlined words, or parts of words, are given greater emphasis as a result.

> Dove sono i bei momenti
> Di dolcezza, e di piacer,
> Dove andaro i giuramenti
> Di quel labbro menzogner, di quel labbro menzogner?
> Perchè mai, se in pianti e in pene
> Per me tutto si cangiò,
> La memoria di quel bene
> Dal mio sen non trapassò,
> La memoria di quel ben non trapassò?
> Dove sono i bei momenti
> Di dolcezza, e di piacer,
> Dove andaro i giuramenti
> Di quel labbro menzogner ...

CASSETTE 2, SIDE 2, ITEM 11

Aria: second part

We're now going to complete our work on this piece by considering the second part of the aria, the quicker part. Read through the words first of all (they are given below) and notice the glimmer of hope that shines through. Then listen to them as Item 11. What are the main musical changes that Mozart has made in this part in order to match the meaning of the words? Comment on tempo, melodic shape and the role of the orchestra.

Ah, se almen la mia costanza
Nel languire amando ognor,
Mi portasse una speranza
Di cangiar l'ingrato cor,
Di cangiar l'ingrato cor,
Ah, se almen la mia costanza
Ah, se almen la mia costanza
Nel languire amando ognor,
Mi portasse una speranza
Di cangiar l'ingrato cor,
Mi portasse una speranza
Di cangiar l'ingrato cor,
Di cangiar l'ingrato cor,
Di cangiar l'ingrato cor,
Di cangiar l'ingrato cor,
L'ingrato cor, l'ingrato cor!

Ah, if only my longing devotion
In despair still strong as before,
Might bring me some expectation
Of changing that faithless heart.
Of changing ...

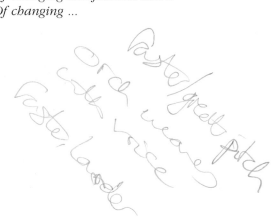

DISCUSSION

Here the Countess is showing signs of hope that her devotion to her husband may change his habits of infidelity. The music is correspondingly much more determined, with a quicker tempo. The melody line uses wider-ranging pitches, and the expressive leaning of the first part of the aria now gives way to faster runs and some more striking higher notes. The orchestra in this second part is more prominent, finishing the aria with a bold flourish.

This aria is a good example of the ways in which formal elements contribute to meaning. The sentiments expressed in words are matched in the music within a coherent, two-part structure; melody in particular is used for expressive purposes, whether to highlight poignancy or to show renewed determination and hope.

Summary

1   Melody may be used for expressive effect, and in this case is both poignant and determined.

2   Composers often make use of standard formulae.

PIECES 5A AND 5B
CAPRICE NO.1, BY PAGANINI
GRANDES ÉTUDES DE PAGANINI
(NO.4), BY LISZT

The performer and music

So far we've discussed pieces of music primarily in terms of their component elements, and we have made little reference to the performer or to the performance situation, save for the discussion of the intimate performance of the Hildegard of Bingen extract. This is an issue that does need to be addressed. After all, for many listeners the performer is the embodiment of the music, often becoming far more famous than the music he or she performs.

EXERCISE

I'd now like you to engage in a somewhat different exercise from the previous ones. Below are three extracts, labelled 1–3, concerning the concept of 'performance'. Two of these are by composers – Aaron Copland and Igor Stravinsky. The third is by the pianist Alfred Brendel. I'd like you to read these three passages and then draw on them to write down answers to the following questions.

According to the authors:

1   What, briefly, is the role of the performer in bringing to life a piece of notated music?

2   What are some of the main differences between a live performance and a recording?

1   Aaron Copland

...the situation of the musical interpreter is not so very different from that of the creator. He [sic] is simply the intermediary that brings the composer's works to life – a kind of midwife to the composition. He partakes of the same dedication of purpose, the same sense of self-discovery through each performance, the same conviction that something unique is lost, possibly, when his own understanding of a work of art is lost. He even partakes of the involuntary nature of creation, for we know that he cannot at will turn on the wellsprings of his creativity so that each performance may be of equal value. Quite the contrary, each time he steps out upon the concert platform we wish him luck, for he shares something of the creator's uncertain powers of projection. Thus we see that interpretation, even though it may rightfully be thought of as an auxiliary art, does share elements of creativity with the mind that forms the work of art.

(Copland, 1952, p.42)

2 Igor Stravinsky

It is taken for granted that I place before the performer written music wherein the composer's will is explicit and easily discernible from a correctly established text. But no matter how scrupulously a piece of music may be notated, no matter how carefully it may be insured against every possible ambiguity through the indications of *tempo*, shading, phrasing, accentuation, and so on, it always contains hidden elements that defy definition, because verbal dialectic is powerless to define musical dialectic in its totality. The realization of these elements is thus a matter of experience and intuition, in a word, of the talent of the person who is called upon to present the music.

(Stravinsky, 1942, p.123)

3 Alfred Brendel

In a concert one plays just once, in the studio several times if necessary. In a concert you must convince the audience at once; in the studio it is the accumulated result that counts.

In a concert the performance is only experienced once; in the studio it can be reproduced. In a concert the performer must get to the end of the piece without a chance to make corrections. In the studio he can make corrections, learn while he records and get rid of nerves.

The player before the public must do four things at the same time: he must imagine the performance, play it, project it and listen to it. In the studio he has the opportunity to hear it again after playing, and to react accordingly.

In a concert it is the broad sweep that counts. The studio demands control over a mosaic; while it offers the performer the possibility of gradually loosening up, there is also the danger of diminishing freshness. And there is the painful business of choosing between takes.

When playing before the public, details must be projected to the furthest ends of the auditorium, just as the whispers of an actor must be heard throughout the theatre. In front of the microphone one tries, on the contrary, to get away from the exaggerations and aims for an interpretation that will bear frequent hearing.

In the concert hall the concentration of the audience brings about a mutual influence between the performer and his listeners. In the studio nobody has to be conquered – but there is nobody to disturb you. The player sits as though in a tomb.

A fit of coughing or the chirping of the alarm on a watch may break the spell of the most delicate moment of the concert. The studio offers silence.

Weaknesses in a concert performance tend to result from spontaneity, from a break in concentration or from nervous pressure. In the studio they may have their roots in excessive critical awareness.

The ability to convince the public in the concert hall is quite independent of absolute perfection. The studio is ruled by the aesthetics of compulsive cleanliness.

(Brendel, 1995, pp.200–1)

DISCUSSION

1   There are many points of interest in these articles, but the central issue seems to be that the performer is essential in bringing to life a notated piece of music. According to Copland, the performer is a vital part of the composition process itself, bringing something new to the work each time that it is played. Stravinsky raises the matter of the fallibility of the written item, which can never contain every detail essential to a performance.

2   Brendel highlights the fact that a performance is unique and cannot be recreated. He refers to the interaction between the performer and the listener and says that a convincing performance need not be a flawless one, though a recording studio gives the performer the opportunity to repeat a piece until it is accurate.

These passages all refer to the relationship between notated music and its realization in performance, which commonly takes place in a formal environment such as a concert hall. There are, of course, other environments which would raise different issues. In TV3 you see a performance in a pub session in Ireland. Here there is no notated music, and the ambience of the venue significantly affects the musical performance.

The venue itself contributes to the success of the performance of a particular piece: what works well in Wembley Stadium will not necessarily be appropriate in a small, confined space. In TV13 you will look at performance and 'style', and in Study Week 29 you will be introduced to the concept of 'authentic' performance.

The three passages that you've just read refer to the responsibilities of the performer in the realization of a piece of music that is notated. But what about the personal qualities of individual performers – their different natures and abilities? How might these factors affect the very composition of a piece of music?

CASSETTE 2, SIDE 2, ITEM 12

Listen now to Item 12, which is a short piece for violin. Jot down a few words that describe the sorts of demand this makes on the player. Do you think that it is technically challenging? You might try to recall some of the violin passages from the Stravinsky extract to help you.

DISCUSSION

The terms I thought of were 'brilliant', 'glittering', 'wide-ranging', 'fast'. This is an exceptionally demanding piece that was written for a **virtuoso** player (one who has phenomenal technical skills and a thorough command of the instrument). It requires the player to be able to play very rapid passages that cover the whole range of the instrument, especially the highest notes. There is a large amount of difficult, swiftly executed double-stopping.

The piece was actually written for the violin by a violinist, Nicolò Paganini. Paganini was an extraordinary and highly influential figure, who was famous in the early part of the nineteenth century, not only for his technical wizardry but also for his sheer magnetism as a performer. Paganini conceived this piece as one of twenty-four **caprices**. These are really studies, pieces of music originally designed not to be played in public but to stretch the violinist to the limit. Paganini admitted that he had deliberately invented difficulties in order to work out how to master them, demanding more and more arduous finger techniques (in the left hand) as well as requiring tremendous agility and dexterity in the bowing (right) arm.

FIGURE 3.13
Sir Edwin Landseer,
Nicolò Paganini,
*1840. (Mansell
Collection)*

CASSETTE 2, SIDE 2, ITEM 13

Now listen to Item 13. How is this related to Item 12?

DISCUSSION

I hope that you were able to hear that this was the same piece, but this time for piano instead of violin. Paganini's influences were not restricted to violinists. For the piano virtuoso, Franz Liszt, he was inspirational. Like Paganini, Liszt was a performer of extraordinary charisma who stretched his instrument to its limits, writing music to explore the piano's technical potential and enormous timbral variety. Hearing Paganini perform live in 1831, Liszt was inspired to rework six of his caprices for piano solo, one of which you have just heard.

It is still widely acknowledged that Liszt was one of the greatest pianists of all time, and that he wrote music that places enormous demands on the performer. This is how the composer Robert Schumann described one of Liszt's 1840 concerts in Dresden:

> There was a roar of acclaim as he entered. And then he began to play.
>
> I had already heard him, but privately. It is one thing to hear an artist playing for a few friends, quite another to hear him before an audience. It is a different occasion – and a different artist. The beautiful, bright rooms, illuminated by candlelight, the bejewelled and decorated audience, all stimulate the giver as well as the given. The demon began to flex his muscles. He first played along with them, as if to feel them out, and then gave them a taste of something more substantial until, with his magic, he had ensnared each and every one and could move them this way or that as he chose.
>
> It is unlikely that any other artist, excepting only Paganini, has the power to lift, carry and deposit an audience in such high degree. A Viennese writer has celebrated Liszt in a poem consisting of nothing but adjectives beginning with the individual letters of his name. It is a tasteless thing as poetry, but there is something to be said for it. Just as we are overwhelmed in leafing through a dictionary by an onslaught of letters and definitions, so in listening to Liszt are we overwhelmed by an onslaught of sounds and sensations. In a matter of seconds we have been exposed to tenderness, daring, fragrance and madness. The instrument glows and sparkles under the hands of its master. This has all been described a hundred times, and the Viennese, in particular, have tried to trap the eagle in every possible way – with winged pursuit, with snares, with pitchforks and with poems. It simply has to be heard – and seen. If Liszt were to play behind the scenes, a considerable portion of poetry would be lost.
>
> (Schumann: Pleasants (ed.), 1965, p.157)

The piece of virtuosic music in Items 12/13, written to show off the technical prowess of the player, was just one of many examples that I

A musical experience is an interaction between composer, performer + listener, all are vital.

could have chosen for discussion in this section. The concept of 'performance' is a subject to which you will return throughout the course, not only with regard to music but also to drama. In Block 5 you will look at plays in performance, and in Block 6 one of the themes will be the performance of music in the 1960s. What I hope you will now take away from this section is the awareness that a musical experience is an interaction between composer, player (or singer) and listener, all of whom play a vital role in the performance process. *In the words of composer Benjamin Britten (1964, p.13)*, 'Music does not exist in a vacuum, it does not exist until it is performed ...'

Summary

1   The performance of a piece of music requires the participation of composer, performer and listener.

2   Notated music needs a performer to bring it to life.

3   The performance environment can influence the performance.

4   Some music is written specifically to show off the virtuosity of the player.

PIECE 6
'SONGS FROM THE WOOD', BY JETHRO TULL

Textures/words/performance

The last piece for study this week offers you an opportunity to draw together some of your earlier work as we examine a song by the group Jethro Tull. This song has been chosen because of its rich, varied textures. If you think back to Piece 1, you will recall that 'texture' refers to the combining of melodies, rhythms and timbres to create different thicknesses of sound. It may help you to understand this term if you relate it to the idea of texture in fabric. 'Texture' is derived from the Latin verb *texere*, 'to weave'. Different fabrics have different 'weaves'. In an Aran knit, for example, you can see strands of wool woven together, some of them moving in opposite directions. Sometimes pieces of music have a similar interweaving of strands, with separate melodic lines played concurrently, weaving against one another in what is known as **counterpoint**. At other times, notes move simultaneously, creating chordal textures (a **chord** is the simultaneous combination of several notes).

CASSETTE 2, SIDE 2, ITEM 14

Listen to Item 14, a description of different textures, with short musical illustrations.

CASSETTE 2, SIDE 2, ITEM 15

This exercise is an initial listening exercise to guide you into the complex and varied textures of 'Songs from the Wood'. Figure 3.14 gives four choices of texture, A–D (with some information on the timbres that contribute to these textures). Study this first.

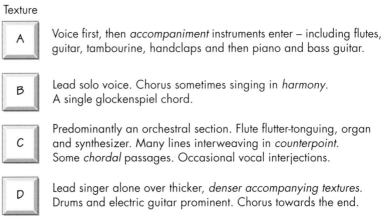

Texture

A Voice first, then *accompaniment* instruments enter – including flutes, guitar, tambourine, handclaps and then piano and bass guitar.

B Lead solo voice. Chorus sometimes singing in *harmony*. A single glockenspiel chord.

C Predominantly an orchestral section. Flute flutter-tonguing, organ and synthesizer. Many lines interweaving in *counterpoint*. Some *chordal* passages. Occasional vocal interjections.

D Lead singer alone over thicker, *denser accompanying textures*. Drums and electric guitar prominent. Chorus towards the end.

FIGURE 3.14 *Key to textures*

Now look at Figure 3.15, which shows you the words of the song, with six blank boxes alongside. Your task will be to listen to the song in Item 15 and enter a letter into each blank box in Figure 3.15 to describe the texture of different parts of the song. Write the one letter (A, B, C or D) that you feel describes what you are hearing.

(Listen to the song – Item 15 – as often as you like, and refer back to Figure 3.14 to remind yourself of the textures.)

| | Words | Texture |

Let me bring you Songs from the Wood,
To make you feel much better than you could know,
Dust you down from tip to toe,
Show you how the garden grows,
Hold you steady as you go,
Hold steady as you join the chorus if you can,
It'll make of you an honest man.

Let me bring you love from the fields,
Poppies red and roses filled with summer rain,
To heal the wound, to still the pain,
To threaten to gain and to gain,
As you drag down every lover's lane,
Life's long celebrations here,
I'll toast you all in penny cheer.

Let me bring you all things refined,
Galliards and lute songs served in chilling ale,
Greetings, well-met fellow, hail!
I am the wind to fill your sail,
I am the cross to take your nail,
A singer of these ageless times,
With kitchen prose, and gutter rhymes.

Songs from the Wood make you feel much better,
Songs from the Wood . . .

Let me bring you love from the fields,
Poppies red and roses filled with summer rain,
To heal the wound, to still the pain,
To threaten to gain and to gain,
As you drag down every lover's lane,
Life's long celebrations here,
I'll toast you all in penny cheer.

Songs from the Wood make you feel much better,
Songs from the Wood make you feel much better.

FIGURE 3.15

DISCUSSION

You should have entered the letters in the order BADCAC. (If you did not get this right, listen again to the cassette.) I hope that this initial listening exercise helped you to hear that there are different textures in the song, both chordal and contrapuntal (the adjective from the word 'counterpoint'), which contribute to the overall effect of variety and balance. We're now going to undertake some more detailed work on each section of the song.

CASSETTE 2, SIDE 2, ITEM 16

The words of the first verse, complete with all the repeated lines, are shown below. This verse is for a solo voice and chorus (in this instance, a group of voices), with a very brief **glockenspiel** interjection at the end of the second line (a glockenspiel is a pitched percussion instrument made of metal) and two flutes at the very end of the verse. The voices are used to provide a mixture of textures: sometimes there is just a single line, and sometimes the voices sing in harmony. Listen to Item 16, Verse 1 of the song. Your task is to underline the lines, or parts of the lines, where the chorus is heard:

> Let me bring you Songs from the Wood,
> To make you feel much better than you could know,
>   better than you could know,
> Dust you down from tip to toe,
>   dust you down from tip to toe,
> Show you how the garden grows,
>   show you how the garden grows,
> Hold you steady as you go,
> Hold steady as you join the chorus if you can,
> It'll make of you an honest man.

DISCUSSION

What happens is that sometimes the chorus simply joins in with the lead singer, but at other times provides an answering, overlapping phrase. The verse begins with a single voice and ends with soloist and chorus together, with answering phrases in the central part of the verse. My detailed answer to this exercise is printed at the end of the unit, as Figure 3.18.

CASSETTE 2, SIDE 2, ITEM 17

We're now going to examine Verse 2 more closely. Figure 3.16 shows you the words of this verse, with the main instruments given at the top of the figure and some questions set within the figure. Listen to Verse 2 (Item 17) and answer the questions in Figure 3.16.

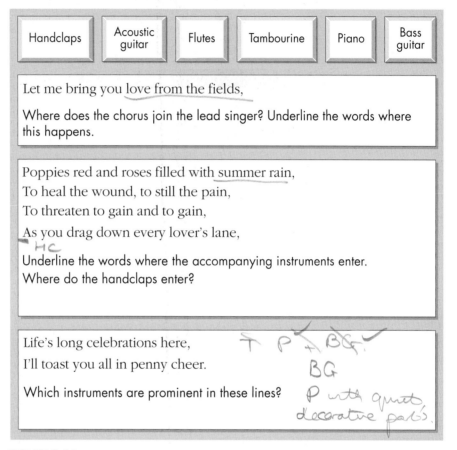

FIGURE 3.16

DISCUSSION

My answer is given as Figure 3.19, at the end of the unit.

So you now have some idea of how textures (and timbres) are working in the first two verses of the song. Verse 1 uses voices only, alternating a single melody line with chords. Verse 2 is more complex, starting with some new accompaniment instruments and ending with quite a dense texture. To achieve this texture, some instruments are given accompanying chords or rhythms, while others (such as the flutes and the piano) have counter-melodies. (Counter-melodies are melodic lines that are not the main melody line, but interweave within the texture as a whole.)

CASSETTE 2, SIDE 2, ITEM 18

I'm not going to ask you questions about Verse 3 and the following instrumental section, but instead am going to talk you through it. First, read my commentary below.

Here, as a reminder, are the words of Verse 3 (for 'galliard' and 'lute song', see the glossary):

> Let me bring you all things refined,
> Galliards and lute songs served in chilling ale,
> Greetings, well-met fellow, hail!
> I am the wind to fill your sail,
> I am the cross to take your nail,
> A singer of these ageless times,
> With kitchen prose, and gutter rhymes.

In this verse the texture continues to thicken. The first noticeable change is that instead of the chorus entering at the end of the first line, this time instruments replace the chorus. Added to the texture in this verse are electric guitar and synthesized keyboard parts, sounding like a harpsichord – a keyboard instrument that was very popular in the eighteenth century. The drumkit takes on a more prominent role in Verse 3.

This denser sound paves the way for a long instrumental passage in which you can hear the flute playing, using a technique called **flutter-tonguing**. The synthesized sounds are developed and an organ joins the texture. Lines interweave within a complex mesh of sound:

> Songs from the Wood make you feel much better,
> Songs from the Wood ...

Finally you hear Verse 4, a repeat of Verse 2:

> Let me bring you love from the fields,
> Poppies red and roses filled with summer rain,
> To heal the wound, to still the pain,
> To threaten to gain and to gain,
> As you drag down every lover's lane,
> Life's long celebrations here,
> I'll toast you all in penny cheer.

Now that you have read my commentary, listen to Item 18 (which consists of Verse 3, the instrumental section and Verse 4), reading through the commentary again as you listen.

CASSETTE 2, SIDE 2, ITEM 19

Complete your work on textures in this song by listening to the closing passage, Item 19 on the cassette. Describe some of the different textures in this section – for example, chords, counterpoint, etc. The only words heard in this section are:

> Songs from the Wood make you feel much better,
> Songs from the Wood make you feel much better.

DISCUSSION

The closing passage returns to denser textures. The flute is highlighted at the beginning of this section, where the textures are quite contrapuntal and include a number of accompaniment figures that use a variety of **motifs** (a motif is a small rhythmic or melodic pattern). The ending is chordal, with a series of short, brisk, chords.

Now read a description, by Allan Moore, of texture in this song. He sees the song as using space to good effect, with a skilful, graded build-up of textures through Verses 1–3. Moore uses the term 'sound-box' to indicate the spectrum of sounds used in this song:

> Jethro Tull's 'Songs from the Wood' represents a ... conceptual advance, as sounds can be considered *placed* in this virtual textural space. The opening consists of solo voice backed with parallel voices, but the subtle glockenspiel and flute fills immediately suggest a greater space than that occupied by the voices alone. A variety of conventional timbres are involved: clapping, tambourine, registrally high organ and guitar, gradually filling out the space and thereby expanding the listener's awareness of how much more may be available, until kit and bass finally enter. The texture has gradually spread from a small centre (which was at the time self-contained) to the whole sound-box. The subsequent use of harpsichord, mandolin and electric guitar is quite subtle, but timbres are sufficiently separated to allow them all to be distinguished.
>
> *(Moore, 1993, p.107)*

CASSETTE 2, SIDE 2, ITEM 20

We have looked at some of the interesting formal aspects of the song, especially its textures. For a discussion of the song and issues relating to it, listen now to Item 20, which is an interview with the composer and lead singer, Ian Anderson. You might like to take a break before you do this as the interview is quite long. ■

FIGURE 3.17   *Jethro Tull (Ian Anderson) in performance. (Photograph: Redferns/David Redfern)*

Summary

1   Pieces of music use different textures or 'thicknesses'.

2   In this song there are both chordal and contrapuntal textures, and a variety of timbres.

3   The listener is a vital part of a performance.

CODA

The main aim of this unit has been to help you develop keener listening skills. In all the pieces studied this week, sound is organized into patterns according to a particular composer's technical and expressive needs. The six pieces that you have studied make their impact through the composer's distinctive manipulation of the elements of music – rhythm, pitch, timbre and texture – within some sort of structure.

This week's work will form the basis of study for your work in Week 22, in which you will look at the ways in which composers use the elements of music in order to express an emotion and to portray characters and events.

GLOSSARY

accompaniment supporting, subordinate part.

afoxê (pronounced 'a-fo-shay') rhythm, with roots in West African religion, that is now particularly popular in Bahia (north-east Brazil around the city of Salvador). It is mainly played by the black carnival associations called Afro Blocos. The Afro Blocos often live together as communities and play drums for carnival and other parades.

aria 'air' or 'tune' – a song in an **opera**.

brass instruments made of brass in which the sound is produced by a cup- or funnel-shaped mouthpiece. Orchestral brass include trumpet, French horn, trombone and tuba.

caprice lively, light piece.

chord sound created by the simultaneous combination of different notes.

Classical Western art music written between the latter part of the eighteenth century and the early part of the nineteenth century; 'classical', without a capital letter, refers to Western art music in general (for example, the piece by Liszt studied in this unit).

counterpoint weaving together of independent melodic lines; the related adjective is 'contrapuntal'.

double-stopping technique by which a string player sounds more than one note at a time.

dynamics indications of levels of loudness for the performer.

ensemble small group

étude study – a piece written to train or demonstrate the facility of the performer, but sometimes having artistic value as well.

flutter-tonguing method of tonguing on a woodwind or a brass instrument in which the player has to roll the letter R while blowing.

galliard simple dance in triple time.

glissando slide.

glockenspiel percussion instrument with tuned metal bars; see also **percussion**.

harmony combination of notes.

lute song song for voice and lute, and possibly a third instrument, very popular in the late sixteenth century and early seventeenth century; the lute is a fretted, plucked string instrument.

melismatic adjective derived from 'melisma', a term used of passages in which one syllable is sung over more than one note.

melody succession of notes having a recognizable musical shape.

metre division of time into regular patterns – for example, four beats in a bar of music.

motif small melodic or rhythmic unit that may be used as the basis for a piece of music.

mute device to dampen and alter the sound of an instrument.

neume dot, dash or curve indicating the shape and direction of the **melody**, as used in neumatic notation.

opera drama set to music. Like a play, an opera is divided into acts and scenes; within a scene there may be solos or **ensembles**.

orchestra grouping together of instruments into a larger body. The actual make-up of the orchestra has changed with the period: Mozart's orchestra was very different from the one used by Stravinsky.

percussion instruments that are sounded by being struck. These may be of definite pitch (for example, tubular bells) or of indefinite pitch (for example, tambourine). In the Jethro Tull song, you heard a **glockenspiel**.

phrase short, distinct part of a **melody**.

pitch highness or lowness of a note.

pizzicato 'plucked'; the strings (for example, of a violin) are plucked with the fingers rather than played with the bow.

register particular part of an instrument's compass.

rhythm way in which sounds are distributed over time; music often has a regular beat, or pulse.

strings 'strings' commonly denotes the orchestral string instruments, which include violins, violas, cellos and double basses.

structure combination and shaping of the elements of music within a structure.

syncopation displacement of accent onto a beat that is not normally accented.

tempo speed of the beat.

texture ways in which voices and instruments can be combined; the word is derived from *texere*, 'to weave'. Composers may choose to weave melodies together in **counterpoint** or may combine notes simultaneously to form **chords**.

timbre tone-colour, or characteristic sound quality, of an instrument.

trill rapid oscillation between two notes.

unison united sounding of the same note; for example, a unison song is one in which a number of people all sing the same tune (not harmonizing). A rhythmic unison is a passage in which a number of players play the same rhythmic pattern.

virtuoso performer who possesses the highest technical skill. A virtuosic piece requires exceptional technical skill for its performance.

woodwind collective name for those types of wind instrument historically made of wood, either blown directly or by means of a reed. The standard orchestral woodwind section comprises flutes, oboes, clarinets and bassoons.

REFERENCES

BAINES, A. (ed.) (1992) *The Oxford Companion to Musical Instruments*, Oxford, Oxford University Press.

BBC (1986) *Thirteen Steps around Toru Takemitsu*, post-production script (series *From East to West*).

BOWEN, M. (ed.) (1995) *Tippett on Music*, Oxford, Oxford University Press.

BRENDEL, A. (1995) *Music Sounded Out*, London, Robson Books (first published 1990).

BRITTEN, B. (1964) *On Receiving the First Aspen Award*, London, Faber and Faber.

COPLAND, A. (1952) *Music and Imagination*, Oxford, Oxford University Press.

DAVIES, R. (1995) *X-Ray*, London, Penguin.

FORD, A. (1993) *Composer to Composer: conversations about contemporary music*, London, Quartet.

MARTIN, G. (1995) *Summer of Love: the making of Sgt. Pepper*, London, Pan Books.

MOORE, A. (1993) *Rock: the primary text*, Buckingham, Open University Press.

PLEASANTS, H. (ed. and trans.) (1965) *The Musical World of Robert Schumann*, London, Gollancz.

SADIE, S. (ed.) (1980) *The New Grove Dictionary of Music and Musicians*, vol.13, London, Macmillan.

STRAVINSKY, I. (1942) *Poetics of Music*, Cambridge, Mass., Harvard University Press.

STRAVINSKY, I. and CRAFT, R. (1959) *Conversations with Igor Stravinsky*, London, Faber and Faber.

STRAVINSKY, I. and CRAFT, R. (1960) *Memories and Commentaries*, London, Faber and Faber.

ANSWERS TO THE EXERCISES ON ITEMS 16 AND 17

Here is my answer to the exercise on Item 16: the underlinings show where the chorus is heard:

Let me bring you <u>Songs from the Wood</u>,
<u>To make you feel much better than you could know</u>,
        <u>better than you could know</u>,
Dust you down from tip to toe,
        <u>dust you down from tip to toe</u>,
Show you how the garden grows,
        <u>show you how the garden grows</u>,
Hold you steady as you go,
<u>Hold steady as you join the chorus if you can</u>,
<u>It'll make of you an honest man</u>.

FIGURE 3.18

Let me bring you <u>love from the fields,</u>

Where does the chorus join the lead singer? Underline the words where this happens.

Poppies red and roses filled with <u>summer rain,</u>
To heal the wound, to still the pain,
To threaten to gain and to gain,
As you drag down every lover's lane,

Underline the words where the accompanying instruments enter.
Where do the handclaps enter?

The handclaps come in just after the words 'to gain and to gain'.

Life's long celebrations here,
I'll toast you all in penny cheer.

Which instruments are prominent in these lines?

Bass guitar comes in. There are also quieter, decorative piano patterns.

FIGURE 3.19

ACKNOWLEDGEMENTS

Grateful acknowledgement is made to the following for permission to reproduce material in this unit:

Text

Veloso, C. 'Um Canto de Afoxé Para o Bloco do Ilê', *Cores Nomes*, Warner/Chappell Music Ltd by permission of IMP Ltd.

Kirby, E. directed by Page, C. 1982, 'O presul vere civitatis', *A feather on the breath of God: sequences and hymns by Abbess Hildegard of Bingen, Gothic voices*, Hyperion Records Limited.

From Mozart, W.A. *The Marriage of Figaro*, Dover Publications Inc. 1979.

'Songs from the Wood', words and music by Ian Anderson. © Copyright 1977 Salamander & Son Music Limited/Chrysalis Music Limited, The Chrysalis Building, Bramley Road, London, W10. Used by permission of Music Sales Limited. All rights reserved. International copyright secured.

UNIT 4 REASONING

Written for the course team by Nigel Warburton

Contents

STUDY COMPONENTS				
Weeks of study	Texts	TV	AC	Set books
1	*Resource Book 1*	TV4	–	–

Aims

The aims of this unit are to:

1   explain what philosophy is;

2   introduce and put into practice some basic skills of argument analysis;

3   provide exercises in critical reading;

4   examine moral questions about euthanasia, animal rights and the move to ban boxing as examples of philosophical reasoning applied to real issues.

Objectives

By the end of this unit you should be able to:

1   recognize what is distinctive about a philosophical approach to various issues;

2   identify and use some basic tools of argument analysis;

3   read a short philosophical article critically.

Study note

The aim of Unit 4 is to encourage you to engage actively with what you are reading rather than to absorb it passively. The structured analysis of philosophical texts will give you the tools to do this; the exercises will give you feedback on your progress and the chance to put into practice what you have learnt. As with Units 2 and 3, there is a glossary at the end to help you with unfamiliar words.

1 INTRODUCTION

Philosophy is different from many other Arts subjects in that to study it you need to do it. To be an art historian, you needn't paint; to study poetry, you needn't be a poet; you can study music without playing an instrument. Yet to study philosophy you have to engage in philosophical **argument**. Not that you have to operate at the level of the great thinkers of the past; but when you study philosophy, you will be doing the same *sort* of thing as them. You can play football without reaching the level of Pelé, and you can get a great deal of intellectual satisfaction from philosophizing without the originality or brilliance of Wittgenstein. But in both cases you will have to develop some of the skills used by the great practitioners. That's one of the reasons why philosophy can be such a rewarding subject to study.

FIGURE 4.1   *Photograph: Mike Levers/The Open University*

2 WHAT IS PHILOSOPHY?

AGSG, ch.2, sect.3, 'Reading strategically'

The word 'philosophy' is derived from the Greek for 'love of wisdom'. But that isn't particularly helpful in understanding how the word is used now. Philosophy is a subject at the core of most humanities courses. It focuses on abstract questions such as 'Does God exist?', 'Is the world really as it appears to us?', 'How should we live?', 'What is Art?', 'Do we have genuine freedom of choice?', 'What is the mind?', and so on.

These very abstract questions can arise out of our everyday experience. Some people caricature philosophy as a subject with no relevance to life, a subject to be studied from an armchair for purely intellectual satisfaction, the academic equivalent of solving crossword puzzles. But this is a serious misrepresentation of large parts of the subject. For instance, TV4 (*Philosophy in Action: debates about boxing*) shows how the heated debate about whether boxing should be banned can only be answered by addressing important abstract questions. What are the acceptable limits of individual freedom in a civilized country? What are the justifications for paternalism, for forcing people to behave in a particular way for their own good? In other words, this debate is not simply about gut reactions to the sport, but depends on fundamental philosophical **assumptions**.

Participants in TV4 give reasons for their positions. The analysis of reasons and arguments is a particular province of philosophy and the focus of this unit. In fact, inasmuch as philosophy has a distinctive method, it is this: the construction, criticism and analysis of arguments. Philosophical skills are applicable in any area where arguments are important, not just in the realms of abstract speculation. They are particularly useful when you are writing essays, since you are usually expected to make a case for your conclusions rather than simply assert them. For this reason, a basic grounding in philosophy is extremely valuable, whatever academic subject you intend to pursue.

3 ARGUMENT STRUCTURE

AGSG, ch.4, sect.3.4, 'Presenting a coherent argument'

We'll begin by looking at the underlying structure of a straightforward argument, the kind of argument that most of us have used or criticized. Then we'll move on to two passages on moral topics: one on **euthanasia** and the other on how we should treat animals. Apart from their intrinsic interest, these passages should give you practice in critical reading and a chance to identify and analyse reasoning techniques.

Argument

First of all it's important to establish what philosophers mean when they talk about arguments. An argument provides reasons or evidence in support of a conclusion. Arguments are very different from mere **assertions**. It is probably easiest to demonstrate this with some examples.

Here is an assertion:

'God doesn't exist'

This is the sort of statement you might hear in ordinary conversation, one that can have profound significance for how you choose to live. But why should anyone believe it? As it stands it is simply an unsupported declaration of one person's belief: it may even be a **prejudice**, a view the speaker has arrived at without bothering to consider reasons or evidence for or against it. The obvious question to ask is 'Why?', 'Why do you believe that God doesn't exist?' As soon as the speaker provides some reasons in support of the view, it ceases to be mere assertion and becomes part of an argument, though not necessarily a good one. Our speaker might back up the initial assertion in this way:

> 'Because if God did exist, then children wouldn't ever die of incurable diseases.'

This statement alone does not lead to the conclusion 'God does not exist'. But in most contexts it would be fairly obvious that the speaker meant you to realize that some children do actually die of incurable diseases. This belief about children dying is unstated, or **implicit**. If we make it **explicit**, then we get:

1   If God did exist, then children wouldn't ever die of incurable diseases.

2   Some children do die of incurable diseases.

3   So God doesn't exist.

(1) and (2) are **premises** from which the conclusion (3) is supposed to follow. Premises are the building blocks of arguments.

So, if we assume for the sake of argument that it is true that if God existed, then children wouldn't die of incurable diseases, *and* that some children do in fact die in this way, does it follow that God doesn't exist? Logically it *does* follow: *if* these two premises are true, then the conclusion (that God doesn't exist) *must* be true. This is one version of what is traditionally known as the Problem of Evil: the problem of how a kind and all-powerful God could allow human suffering given that He, She or It would want to eliminate suffering and also would have the power to do so.

It's important to realize that I'm not saying that God doesn't exist. I'm merely saying that if the two premises are true, then the conclusion that God doesn't exist must be true. You may well believe that the first premise ('If God did exist, then children wouldn't ever die of incurable diseases') is simply false. And if this is what you believe, then there are many people who share this belief. There may be an explanation of why God allows children to die in this way; certainly philosophers of religion have devoted a great deal of energy to finding such an explanation. But what we are doing here is separating the content of the argument from its structure or form. *When analysing the structure of an argument, we put on one side for the time being the question of whether or not the premises are true. Instead we concentrate on the question of whether or not the conclusion really follows from the premises given.*

Notice that the conclusion 'So God doesn't exist' was the first rather than the last thing said. The word 'conclusion' can be slightly confusing because it suggests that it should come at the end, like the conclusion of a story. But in fact, in ordinary discussion, conclusions are often given before the reasons that support them, and are sometimes sandwiched between reasons. When analysing an argument, however, it is a good idea to rearrange premises and conclusion so that their relationship can be seen clearly.

Content and form

Perhaps it's easier to understand the distinction between content and form of arguments if you consider another argument with the same underlying form as the one above:

If the thief had escaped through your garden, there'd be footprints in the flower-bed.

There are no footprints in the flower-bed.

So the thief did not escape through your garden.

Like the previous argument, if the premises are true, then the conclusion must be true. You can question whether or not the premises are true (for instance, you might think that the thief *could* have got away through your garden without leaving any footprints in the flower-bed). But if they are true, then the structure of the argument is such that it follows that it's true that the thief did not escape through your garden.

Sometimes a conclusion is indicated by words such as 'therefore', 'so', 'it follows that' or something similar. However, this isn't always the case. Often these words are left out because the structure of the argument is fairly obvious and doesn't need to be signposted. Similarly, in some contexts you can leave out a premise that is strictly necessary for the argument. For instance, if I said:

Grasshoppers are insects.

So they have six legs.

it is fairly obvious that I intended you to realize that I believe the unstated premise

All insects have six legs.

even though I hadn't spelt that out. With more complicated arguments, it is often a good idea to make explicit any such unstated premises so that the underlying structure of the argument becomes clear. To make sure you've grasped the idea of implicit premises, try the following exercise.

EXERCISE ONE

What is the unstated premise in each of 1–5 below? For each one, write out your answers in the following form:

Unstated premise:

Stated premise:

Conclusion:

1   Fred is a cat, so of course he likes tuna fish.

2   Your car tyres are bald, so your car will never pass the MOT.

3   George Eliot was a woman, so she was mortal.

4   Studying philosophy helps to improve your thinking skills. So you should study philosophy.

5   I think, therefore I exist.

Now check your answers against those on p.170. ■

Truth and validity

AGSG, ch.2, sect.3.5, 'What if you get stuck?'

We looked earlier at the following argument:

If God did exist, then children wouldn't ever die of incurable diseases.

Some children do die of incurable diseases.

So God doesn't exist.

This is a valid argument. If the premises are true, then the conclusion must be true. Philosophers use the words '**valid**' and '**invalid**' only to refer to the structure of *arguments*. An argument cannot be true or false; it can only be valid or invalid. On the other hand, statements, conclusions, assertions, assumptions and premises may be true or false. This use of language differs from everyday uses of the words 'valid' and 'invalid': you will quite often hear people say 'that's a valid point' or 'that view is invalid'. What the speaker means in each case is 'what you said is true' and 'that view is false'. There is a great difference between validity and truth.

A valid argument has a structure that guarantees a true conclusion provided you feed in true premises. It is 'truth-preserving'. You could visualize it as a kind of ticket machine, like the machine that gives you tickets for the Underground. Its machinery is such that (assuming that it is working properly), if you insert genuine coins (= true premises), then you are guaranteed to get a ticket (= a true conclusion). If, however, you use counterfeit money (= false premises), you may or may not get a ticket (= true conclusion); you certainly couldn't be certain of getting a ticket.

For instance, in the argument we've been examining, if the premises are true, then the conclusion that God doesn't exist must be true. If you said that the assumption and premises were true and also that the conclusion was false, you would be contradicting yourself. It would be like saying, 'London is the capital city of England; but London isn't the capital city of England'. However, if one or both of the premises are false, there is no guarantee that the conclusion is true, despite the argument's validity. The question of whether or not an argument is valid can be addressed separately from the question of whether or not its premises and conclusion are true. The question of validity is about the form of the argument; the question of the truth of premises and conclusion is about its content.

Philosophers are particularly keen to present valid arguments with true premises since that's the best way of guaranteeing true conclusions. They use the word '**sound**' to describe any valid argument with true premises (and therefore, also, a true conclusion).

EXERCISE TWO

At this point it is worth pausing to revise some of the key terms introduced so far. The following exercise is meant to give you feedback on your understanding of the material and to give you a chance to put into practice what you've learnt. Don't be discouraged if you don't get the right answers first time around: use the answers and explanations at the end of the unit to help you revise the material covered.

1   *Underline the conclusion in each of the following arguments:*

    (a) Vegetarians don't eat animals. Prawns are animals. I eat prawns. I'm not a vegetarian.

    (b) Your party cannot win the next election. The only way to win an election is to reduce taxation. Your party won't reduce taxation.

2   *Which of the following are valid arguments?*

    (a) Vegetarians don't eat animals. Peanuts are animals. So vegetarians don't eat peanuts.

    (b) All humans are mortal. Flamingos are birds. So flamingos are mortal.

    (c) Anyone who buys a lottery ticket has a small chance of winning. My sister has bought a lottery ticket. So she has a small chance of winning.

    (d) All forms of killing are morally wrong. Capital punishment is a form of killing. Therefore capital punishment is morally wrong.

3 *Match the following terms with the appropriate definitions, (a)–(h).*

argument *g*
assertion *d*
prejudice *e*
conclusion *f*
implicit assumption *a*
sound argument *h*
premise *c*
valid argument *b*

(a) an unstated premise

(b) a structure that guarantees a true conclusion if the premises are true

(c) a statement from which an argument's conclusion is derived

(d) a statement given without providing any reasons or supporting evidence

(e) a belief that is formed without considering evidence for or against it

(f) a statement derived from premises and from which it follows

(g) reasons leading to a conclusion

(h) a valid argument with true premises. ■

A formal fallacy

AGSG, ch.2, sects 2.3 and 2.4, 'Academic language' and 'Academic writing style'

Like the word 'valid', 'fallacy' is used in a technical way by philosophers. In ordinary conversation you often hear people say 'That's a fallacy', meaning simply that what someone has just said is untrue. However, when philosophers use the word 'fallacy' they usually mean that **an argument is invalid**. A fallacy in the strict sense, usually known as a **formal fallacy**, is an invalid argument. An example should clarify this.

Consider the following argument:

All punks wear safety-pins.

Johnny Rotten wears safety-pins.

So Johnny Rotten must be a punk.

Is this a valid argument? Well, at first glance you might take it to be so. One reason for this is that the structure seems quite close to a well-worn example of a valid argument:

All men are mortal.

Socrates was a man.

So Socrates was mortal.

However, if the punk example had precisely the same form, then it would look like this:

> All punks wear safety-pins.
>
> Johnny Rotten is a punk.
>
> So Johnny Rotten wears safety-pins.

In fact the argument

> All punks wear safety-pins.
>
> Johnny Rotten wears safety-pins.
>
> So Johnny Rotten must be a punk.

is an *invalid* one: it is an example of a fallacy. The conclusion does not follow logically from the premises, regardless of whether or not the conclusion happens to be true. The conclusion is a **non sequitur** (Latin for 'it does not follow'). This is because the way the supposed argument is structured allows for the fact that someone can wear safety-pins and yet not be a punk. One way of understanding this is by thinking in terms of a diagram (Figure 4.2).

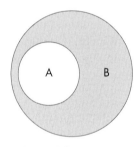

FIGURE 4.2

Circle A stands for the class of punks and circle B for the class of all safety-pin wearers. As you can see, circle A is within circle B, but there is still the possibility of being in circle B without being in circle A. So you cannot conclude from the fact that you are in circle B that you *must* also be in circle A. That's why it is a fallacy: the structure of the argument doesn't reliably give true conclusions, even if you always feed in true premises. The argument is invalid.

Here is a second example of the same fallacy:

> All witches keep black cats.
>
> My neighbour keeps a black cat.
>
> So my neighbour must be a witch.

Again you can see that the conclusion would only follow if the first premise read 'All *and only* witches keep black cats'. But it doesn't say that. So regardless of whether or not it is true that my neighbour is a witch, the argument is fallacious: it is an invalid structure, one which is not truth-preserving. Even if the two premises are true, there can still be people who keep black cats who are not witches. This is precisely the kind of faulty reasoning that has fuelled witch-hunts of various kinds in the past. Such witch-hunts, in addition to using faulty reasoning, were based on the (possibly false) premise that witches actually existed. However, more recent 'witch-hunts', such as the anti-Communist campaign implemented by Senator McCarthy in the 1950s in the United States, often committed the fallacy outlined above. The fact that an individual shared some characteristic with known Communists, such as being interested in workers' rights, was taken as conclusive evidence that this person was a Communist. However, just as having a black cat doesn't make you a witch, being interested in workers' rights doesn't make you a Communist, even if all Communists are interested in workers' rights.

EXERCISE THREE

Which of the following are formal fallacies?

1   All great artists have been slightly crazy. I'm slightly crazy, so I'll end up being a great artist.

2   All babies cry. You're a former baby. So you must have cried.

3   If you break the speed limit, you'll get stopped by the police. You've been stopped by the police. So you must have been speeding.

4   Some philosophers are terrible writers. You're not a philosopher. So you must be a good writer.

5   All fish have gills. Dolphins are fish. Therefore dolphins have gills.

The answers are given at the end of the unit.   ■

Deduction and induction

The examples of arguments we have considered so far have all been deductive arguments. Deductive arguments are so constructed that if the premises are true, then the conclusion must be true. However, there is another important type of argument which does not guarantee the truth of the conclusion even if all the premises are true. Inductive arguments are usually based on evidence which by its nature cannot be conclusive: their conclusions can only ever be *probable*, never certain. For instance, the following is an inductive argument:

> All the flamingos I have ever seen were pink.
>
> Therefore all flamingos are pink.

The fact that I have seen quite a few flamingos, and they were all pink, seems to support the conclusion that all flamingos are pink. However, as it only takes one non-pink flamingo to undermine the generalization that all flamingos are pink, I cannot be absolutely sure that every flamingo in the world is pink. For all I know, there are some albino flamingos. If naturalists who have watched flamingos for decades report that they have never seen a flamingo that wasn't pink, this lends further support to my conclusion. Yet even then the slight possibility would remain that a non-pink flamingo might show up. This inductive argument is very different from a deductive one since with a deductive argument, provided that the premises are true, you can be absolutely certain that the conclusion is true. This is not to say that **induction** is to be despised for its unreliability: we happily rely on inductive reasoning every day of our lives.

EXERCISE FOUR

Which of the following are examples of **deduction**? Which of induction?

1   All gods are immortal. Zeus is a god. So Zeus is immortal.

2   The sun has always risen in the past. So it will rise tomorrow.

3   All the students I have ever met enjoyed Open University summer schools. So all students enjoy Open University summer schools.

4   If you add the milk too quickly, the sauce will go lumpy. You added the milk too quickly. So the sauce will go lumpy.

5   All mammals are sensitive to pain. Rats are mammals. Therefore rats are sensitive to pain.

The answers are given at the end of the unit.   ■

EXERCISE FIVE

AGSG, ch.2, sect.5, 'Making notes'

You've now been studying philosophy for at least a couple of hours, but do you have a clear idea what the subject is? Stop and jot down a few notes in answer to the question: *What is philosophy?* It's not an easy question to answer, but try to identify several distinctive features of the subject. If possible, discuss the question with other students.

DISCUSSION

When you've written down your own answer, read B1–B4 in *Resource Book 1* where you will find a range of responses. There is no single right answer to the question: philosophers have at various times disagreed profoundly about the nature of their subject. Thinking about the question yourself, before looking at other people's answers, should have helped to focus your reading.

4 READING PHILOSOPHY

Introduction

AGSG, ch.2, sect.3.2, 'Reading speed'

Reading philosophy is a skill that has to be learnt. To do it well requires more concentration than many other types of reading. It is an active rather than a passive process: you have to think critically about what you are reading as you read it. You need both to understand the author's position, and also to decide whether the author has really put forward a coherent case for that position. This involves analysing arguments. However, the arguments that philosophers use when writing books and articles are often not as clearly stated or as straightforward as the ones we've been considering so far.

In this section of the unit we'll be looking closely at two passages of philosophy: one by a contemporary philosopher, James Rachels; the other by the eighteenth-century philosopher, Jeremy Bentham.

FIGURE 4.3 *Photograph: Mike Levers/The Open University*

Extract 1: Rachels on euthanasia

The following is an extract from James Rachels's article 'Active and passive euthanasia'. The full article is reproduced in *Resource Book 1* (B5), but for the moment you should concentrate on the extract below; you will have the opportunity to read the full article when you come to Exercise Seven. Rachels focuses on an alleged moral distinction between two types of euthanasia performed by doctors. **Active euthanasia is** where a doctor kills a patient, perhaps by injecting a lethal drug, in order to end the patient's suffering. **Passive euthanasia** is where a doctor withholds treatment from a patient who cannot survive without medical aid, and as a result the patient dies.

Rachels is only concerned with the moral issue, not with the legal one. He uses argument to clarify whether or not there is a moral difference between the two sorts of euthanasia.

EXERCISE SIX

Read through the extract two or three times before going on to the questions below. Don't worry if it seems to take you quite a long time to sort out precisely what Rachels's point is. Reading philosophy requires a different sort of concentration from reading a novel and is usually a slower process.

AGSG, ch.2, sect.5.1, 'Highlighting and underlining'

One reason why so many people think that there is an important moral difference between active and passive euthanasia is that they think killing someone is morally worse than letting someone die. But is it? Is killing, in itself, worse than letting die? To investigate this issue, two cases may be considered that are exactly alike except that one involves killing whereas the other involves letting someone die. Then, it can be asked whether this difference makes any difference to the moral assessments. It is important that the cases be exactly alike, except for this one difference, since otherwise one cannot be confident that it is this difference and not some other that accounts for any variation in the assessments of the two cases. So, let us consider this pair of cases:

In the first, Smith stands to gain a large inheritance if anything should happen to his six-year-old cousin. One evening while the child is taking his bath, Smith sneaks into the bathroom and drowns the child, and then arranges things so that it will look like an accident.

In the second, Jones also stands to gain if anything should happen to his six-year-old cousin. Like Smith, Jones sneaks in planning to drown the child in his bath. However, just as he enters the bathroom Jones sees the child slip and hit his head, and fall face down in the water. Jones is delighted; he stands by, ready to push the child's head back under if it is necessary, but it is not necessary. With only a little thrashing about, the child drowns all by himself, 'accidentally', as Jones watches and does nothing.

Now Smith killed the child, whereas Jones 'merely' let the child die. That is the only difference between them. Did either man behave better, from a moral point of view? If the difference between killing and letting die were in itself a morally important matter, one should say that Jones's behaviour was less reprehensible than Smith's. But does one really want to say that? I think not. In the first place, both men acted from the same motive, personal gain, and both had exactly the same end in view when they acted. It may be inferred from Smith's conduct that he is a bad man, although that judgement may be withdrawn or modified if certain further facts are learned about him – for example, that he is mentally deranged. But would not the very same thing be inferred about Jones from his conduct? And would not the same further considerations also be relevant to any modification of this judgement? Moreover, suppose Jones pleaded, in his own defence, 'After all, I didn't do anything except just stand there and watch the child drown. I didn't kill him; I only let him die.' Again, if letting die were in itself less bad than killing, this defence should have at least some weight. But it does not. Such a 'defence' can only be regarded as a grotesque perversion of moral reasoning. Morally speaking, it is no defence at all.

(Resource Book 1, B5, extract)

Now write brief answers to the following questions and then compare your answers with mine at the end of the unit. Try not to look at my answers until after you've written your own. These questions are designed to make sure that you have fully understood the passage:

1   Why, according to Rachels, do some people believe there to be a moral difference between active and passive euthanasia?

2   Which kind of euthanasia is Smith's case meant to parallel?

3   Why has Rachels put inverted commas around the word 'accidentally'?

4   What sort of difference might the knowledge that Smith was mentally deranged make to our assessment of his case?

5   Does Rachels believe there to be an important moral difference between the cases of Smith and Jones?   ■

Three basic questions

Once you are sure that you have understood what an author is saying, there are three basic questions that you should ask yourself whenever you read any philosophy:

1   What is the author's main conclusion?

2   What reasons does he or she give in support of this conclusion?

3   How good is the author's argument?

In order to see how this works in practice, let's apply these questions to Rachels's passage on euthanasia:

1   What is Rachels's main conclusion?

Those who oppose active euthanasia (which involves killing) but defend passive euthanasia (which involves letting die), on the grounds that letting die is always less blameworthy than killing, are misguided. Killing is not in itself more blameworthy than letting die.

2   What reasons does he give in support of this conclusion?

Rachels uses two imaginary cases to support this conclusion. The case of Smith who deliberately drowns a child is meant to be equivalent to active euthanasia; that of Jones who chooses not to intervene when a child in his care is drowning is meant to be equivalent to passive euthanasia. Both act from the same motive (personal gain), and both want the child to die. In both cases the same sorts of consideration about diminished responsibility apply. Furthermore, if there were a moral difference between killing and letting die, we would expect Jones to be able to make a case for himself by pointing out that he did not actively kill the boy, only let him die. But, Rachels says, this wouldn't have any weight, but would be 'a grotesque perversion of moral reasoning'. Since Smith and Jones seem equally morally responsible for a child's death, Rachels concludes there is nothing about killing in itself that makes it morally worse than letting die.

3   How good is his argument?

Rachels's example of Jones makes a convincing case that in at least some contexts we can reasonably be held responsible for things we don't do, as well as for the things that we do. Jones, by refraining from intervening to save the child, did something for which we would hold him morally responsible, even though in a sense he did nothing at all (he just let events take their course). By taking an example that had nothing directly to do with euthanasia, Rachels made clear the underlying conceptual issues about responsibility. By taking an imaginary rather than a real case, he was able to remove the irrelevant details and concentrate on two cases that were identical in every respect except for the question of whether the child was killed or simply allowed to die.

What criticisms can be made of Rachels's argument? One line that might be taken against it is that his examples are far-fetched and differ significantly from typical cases of euthanasia. For example, euthanasia is always performed for the sake of the patient, whereas in Rachels's imagined cases the killing and letting die are both due to selfish motives and are examples of murder rather than euthanasia. In fact, Rachels answers this possible criticism in the paragraph that follows directly from our extract:

Now, it may be pointed out, quite properly, that the cases of euthanasia with which doctors are concerned are not like this at all. They do not involve personal gain or the destruction of normal healthy children. Doctors are concerned only with cases in which the patient's life is of no further use to him, or in which the patient's life has become or will soon become a terrible burden. However, the point is the same in these cases: the bare difference between killing and letting die does not, in itself, make a moral difference. If a doctor lets a patient die, for humane reasons, he is in the same moral position as if he had given the patient a lethal injection for humane reasons.

(Resource Book 1, B5, extract)

Following on from this, you might want to question the fact that he uses **thought experiments** to come to a conclusion on such an important topic. It is important to appreciate the role that thought experiments play in philosophy.

A note on thought experiments

As we have seen, Rachels uses two imaginary cases to support his argument. Such use of examples is typical of philosophical writing. Often these examples are deliberately far-fetched, the sort of thing that you might expect in a science fiction novel. That shouldn't make you treat them less seriously: by eliminating the distracting and irrelevant details of real-life examples, and by exaggerating certain features, philosophers aim to bring out what is really at issue.

For instance, if someone claims 'All that human beings ever want out of life is pleasurable feelings', a philosopher might concoct a thought experiment in order to show that this view is implausible. In thought experiments, as in scientific experiments, conditions are kept controlled so that you can be reasonably sure of the source of your results. Imagine that you could have electrodes plugged into your head for the rest of your life and that these electrodes produced intensely pleasurable feelings for you whenever you pressed a lever. Would you choose to spend the rest of your life in an armchair pressing the lever? Well, you might. But many people wouldn't.

What this thought experiment is intended to reveal is that many of us want more out of life than a succession of blissful mental states, a life of pleasurable feelings. The example is deliberately far-fetched: but that's because it's the best way of making the point. Similarly, even if you find Rachels's examples of Smith and Jones unlikely, this in no way undermines their force in demonstrating that killing and letting die can be equivalent from a moral point of view.

EXERCISE SEVEN

Now that you've looked more closely at Rachels's central argument, try reading the whole of his article, which is included in *Resource Book 1* (B5). Allow yourself plenty of time: as I've already mentioned, most of us find that reading philosophy requires a special kind of concentration.

You may find yourself disagreeing with Rachels's conclusions. If so, try to give reasons for your disagreement. Has he ignored some crucial feature of the situations he describes? Perhaps you feel that he has not given weight to the possible consequences of the legalization of active euthanasia? Or perhaps you want to take issue with the use he makes of his thought experiments? Remember that to read this as philosophy requires your involvement with the ideas. It is not enough simply to absorb what Rachels says: try to engage with it. Philosophy is a living subject, one that thrives on debate and disagreement. Ideally you should discuss the contents of this essay with friends or fellow students.

Even if you find yourself in full agreement with Rachels's position, try thinking through possible objections and how he might meet them. ■

Extract 2: Bentham on the status of animals

The following is an extract from a book by the philosopher Jeremy Bentham (1748–1832). It is a famous passage in which he questions the basis of granting rights to humans but not to animals. Most of the difficulty in making sense of this passage stems from the language: Bentham was writing in the eighteenth century and used several words and phrases that are no longer common (the book from which this extract is taken, *Introduction to the Principles of Morals and Legislation*, was published in 1789). I have added explanations of these in square brackets. As with the previous passage, read this one through several times before moving on to Exercise Eight:

> The day *may* come when the rest of the animal creation may acquire those rights which never could have been witholden [withheld] from them but [except] by the hand of tyranny. The French have already discovered that the blackness of the skin is no reason why human beings should be abandoned without redress to the caprice [whim] of a tormentor [torturer]. It may one day come to be recognized that the number of the legs, the villosity [hairiness] of the skin, or the termination of the *os sacrum*,* are reasons equally insufficient for abandoning a sensitive being [capable of feeling] to the same fate. What else is it that should trace the insuperable line [a division that can't be crossed]? Is it the faculty of reason [ability to reason], or perhaps the faculty of discourse [ability to speak]? But a full-grown horse or dog is beyond comparison a more rational, as well as a more conversable animal [capable of communication], than an infant of a day, or a week, or even a month, old. But suppose they were otherwise,

what would it avail? [what difference would it make?] The question is not, Can they reason? nor Can they *talk?* But *Can they suffer?*

(Bentham, 1789)

* a bone at the end of the backbone, i.e. whether or not an animal has a tail

EXERCISE EIGHT

Summarize the above passage *using no more than 75 words.* Your summary should include only the main points. Compare your summary with mine at the end of the unit. ■

I now want to discuss the same three basic questions that I asked about Rachels's passage:

1   What is the author's main conclusion?

2   What reasons does he give in support of this conclusion?

3   How good is his argument?

1   What is Bentham's main conclusion?

Bentham's main conclusion comes at the end of the passage: it is that the relevant question to ask is not whether animals can reason, or whether they can talk, but whether they can suffer.

2   What reasons does he give in support of this conclusion?

Bentham doesn't offer any reasons directly in support of his conclusion: he simply asserts it. However, he *does* argue against the idea that the ability to reason, or the ability to speak, decides the issue. We'll examine these arguments in more detail below. By eliminating the alternative accounts of the features that determine whether or not an animal deserves rights, Bentham gives indirect support to his conclusion.

3   How good is his argument?

In favour of Bentham's argument it might be thought that, once he has eliminated reason or speech as the appropriate criterion for deciding which animals have rights, there is only one plausible alternative left: the capacity to suffer.

However, against Bentham, we might point out that he has not explained *why* the capacity to suffer is relevant. It is also worth looking in more detail at his comparison between children and other animals. He asks whether we can draw a line between humans and animals on the grounds that humans can reason and speak, and he concludes that we can't. Note that his argument depends on the assumption that children merit rights. Nowhere does he state this explicitly, but it is clear that he takes it for granted and expects his readers to do so too.

Given this assumption, he shows that if we relied solely on ability to reason as the way of distinguishing those that have rights from those that don't, then we would have to give rights to some non-human animals since they have a greater capacity to reason than some new-born children. Similarly, new-born children don't have the ability to speak, and yet some animals can understand and communicate to a certain extent with human beings: so if ability to speak is all that counts, we would probably have to exclude some babies from our category of those animals that merit rights. However, since Bentham assumes (quite reasonably) that all human babies merit rights, this conclusion is unacceptable.

FIGURE 4.4   *Photograph: Hulton Getty Picture Collection*

Reductio ad absurdum

The underlying argument that Bentham uses here takes the form of a *reductio ad absurdum* (literally a reduction to absurdity). This is a technique for showing that a position is false. Here Bentham wants to show that neither capacity to reason nor capacity to speak is relevant to the question of rights. In order to show this, he considers what it would be like if they *were* relevant. He supposes for the sake of argument that they are relevant, and demonstrates the absurd consequences that would then follow logically. Here is the underlying argument:

Implicit assumption: Babies have rights.

Premise: Rights *are* based on capacity to reason or speak.

Premise: Babies can do neither.

Conclusion: So babies don't have rights.

which creates a huge contradiction + ∴ reduces the opposing argument to absurdity

As can be seen, the implicit assumption that babies have rights is directly contradicted by the conclusion that babies don't have rights. Obviously the implicit assumption and the conclusion can't both be true: that would be absurd. So because the argument leads to a **contradiction**, we can conclude that there is something wrong with it, namely that the supposition that rights are based on the ability to reason or speak is simply false.

The important point is that Bentham was offering a **refutation** of the belief that ability to reason or use language determined whether or not an animal had rights. Another way of looking at the same refutation is to see Bentham as pointing out that consistent application of the theory that ability to reason is the most important feature would lead to the consequence that some young babies would not merit rights. This is obviously an unattractive and implausible consequence.

However, you might want to question his comment that some non-human animals are better at communicating than some babies. You might want to reply that most babies have the capacity to develop into sophisticated language-users, but no non-human animal does, and that this is the relevant criterion for drawing a line between those animals that merit rights and those that don't. By talking about actual rather than potential communication, Bentham avoids this issue. So his argument needs to be expanded somewhat to make this a convincing case.

5 CONCLUSION

This unit has introduced some of the basic skills and vocabulary needed for reading and writing philosophy. Obviously much more could be said about each of the topics touched on in the examples: the aim here has been to concentrate on the structure of arguments rather than on the detail of their content. The emphasis throughout has been on argument analysis. This is a central feature of philosophy. Philosophers present arguments; they also analyse and criticize the arguments used by other philosophers. This is how the subject moves forward. As I stressed at the beginning of the unit, in order to read philosophy effectively, you have to think critically about what you're reading. This can be difficult at first, and slow. But the rewards in terms of transferable thinking skills and the intrinsic interest of the subject make it well worth the effort.

REVISION TEST

The multiple-choice questions that follow are intended to give you some feedback on how much of the unit you have absorbed. The answers are at the end of the unit.

Question 1

1   Premises can be valid.

2   Arguments can be sound.

3   Formal fallacies can yield true conclusions.

Which of these three statements is/are true?

(a) 1 only.

(b) 2 only.

(c) 3 only.

(d) 2 and 3 only.

(e) none of the above.

Question 2

1   Fish have gills.

2   Sharks don't have gills.

3   Sharks aren't fish.

4   Fish don't have gills.

Which of the above statements contradict each other?

(a) 1 and 2.

(b) 1 and 3.

(c) 1 and 4.

(d) 3 and 4.

(e) none of the above.

Question 3

1   A sound argument is valid and has true premises.

2   Valid arguments can have false premises.

3   Non sequiturs are the same as contradictions.

Which of the above statements is/are *false?*

(a) 1 only.

(b) 2 only.

(c) 3 only.

(d) 1 and 3 only.

(e) 1, 2 and 3.

Question 4

1 *All men are mortal. Queen Elizabeth the First was a man. Therefore Queen Elizabeth the First was mortal.*

2 *If you can catch a ball on your nose, you must be a seal. You can catch a ball on your nose. So you are a seal.*

3 *All Open University students are highly motivated. You are highly motivated. So you must be an Open University student.*

Which of the above is/are valid?

(a) 1 only.

(b) 2 only.

(c) 3 only.

(d) 1 and 3 only.

(e) 1 and 2 only.

Question 5

'Boxing should be banned because it causes brain damage.'

Which of the following could be an implied premise of the above argument?

1 *All sports that cause brain damage should be banned.*

2 *All sports that cause physical damage to participants should be banned.*

3 *All activities that cause brain damage should be banned.*

(a) 1 only.

(b) 2 only.

(c) 3 only.

(d) 1 and 2 only.

(e) 1, 2 and 3.

Question 6

The main purpose of Rachels's thought experiment is:

(a) to entertain the reader;

(b) to warn of the dangers of bathing children;

(c) to demonstrate that active euthanasia is always more painful than passive;

(d) to undermine the alleged moral distinction between active and passive euthanasia;

(e) to suggest that there is no such thing as passive euthanasia.

Question 7

Bentham believed that:

(a) animals should be treated as badly as, or worse than, slaves;

(b) animals' capacity to suffer was the most relevant consideration when deciding how to treat them;

(c) the ability to talk is what should determine how we treat other creatures;

(d) intelligent animals should be treated better than week-old human babies;

(e) we should give equal moral weight to a full-grown horse and a week-old human baby.

Question 8

1   *Philosophers aren't interested in argument.*

2   *Philosophy has no relevance for any aspect of our lives.*

3   *Philosophy is simply the history of who thought what.*

Which of the above is true?

(a) 1 only.

(b) 2 only.

(c) 3 only.

(d) 2 and 3 only.

(e) none of the above.

GLOSSARY

active euthanasia mercy killing, usually achieved by deliberately administering a lethal dose of a drug.

argument reasons or evidence leading to a conclusion.

assertion unsupported statement.

assumption premise for which no argument is given; one which is accepted for the purposes of the argument.

contradiction saying two things that cannot both be true.

deduction type of argument that always gives true conclusions provided the premises are true.

euthanasia see **active euthanasia** and **passive euthanasia**.

explicit stated.

formal fallacy strictly speaking, an invalid argument; however, the word 'fallacy' is sometimes used in a looser sense to mean any unreliable way of reasoning.

implicit unstated.

induction type of argument which, even if the premises are true, doesn't guarantee the truth of the conclusion; a generalization based on a range of observations.

invalid argument one in which the conclusion does not follow logically from the premises.

non sequitur statement that does not follow logically from what has gone before.

passive euthanasia deliberately letting someone die, usually in order to prevent their further suffering.

prejudice belief formed without weighing the evidence for or against it.

premise statement from which a conclusion is derived.

reductio ad absurdum literally a reduction to absurdity. Strictly speaking it is a technique for showing a position to be false by supposing that the position is true and then demonstrating that this leads to a contradiction.

refutation demonstration that a position is false.

sound argument valid argument with true premises, and so a true conclusion.

thought experiment imaginary situation designed to bring out a particular point.

valid argument one in which the conclusion follows logically from the premises, whether or not the premises and conclusion happen to be true.

REFERENCES

BENTHAM, J. (1789; reprint 1948) *Introduction to the Principles of Morals and Legislation*, New York, Hafner.

SUGGESTIONS FOR FURTHER READING

You are *not* required to read the following as part of your year's work on A103. However, you may find it helpful and interesting to read one or more of them if you wish to pursue an interest beyond your A103 work:

GLOVER, J. (1977) *Causing Death and Saving Lives,* Harmondsworth, Penguin.

NAGEL, T. (1987) *What Does it All Mean? A very short introduction to philosophy,* Oxford, Oxford University Press.

SINGER, P. (ed.) (1986) *Applied Ethics*, Oxford, Oxford University Press.

WARBURTON, N. (1995, 2nd edn) *Philosophy: The Basics*, London, Routledge.

WARBURTON, N. (1996) *Thinking from A to Z*, London, Routledge.

ANSWERS TO EXERCISES

Exercise One

1   Unstated premise: All cats like tuna fish.
     Stated premise: Fred is a cat.
     Conclusion: So of course he likes tuna fish.

2   Unstated premise: If your car tyres are bald, your car will never pass the MOT.
     Stated premise: Your car tyres are bald.
     Conclusion: So your car will never pass the MOT.

3   Unstated premise: All women are mortal.
     Stated premise: George Eliot was a woman.
     Conclusion: So she was mortal.

4   Unstated premise: You should study subjects which help to improve your thinking skills.
     Stated premise: Studying philosophy helps to improve your thinking skills.
     Conclusion: So you should study philosophy.

5   Unstated premise: Everything that thinks exists.
     Stated premise: I think.
     Conclusion: Therefore I exist.

Exercise Two

1   (a)   I'm not a vegetarian.

     (b)   Your party cannot win the next election.

2   (a)   valid (even though one of the premises and the conclusion are false)

     (b)   invalid

     (c)   valid

     (d)   valid

3   a = implicit assumption

     b = valid argument

     c = premise

     d = assertion

     e = prejudice

     f = conclusion

     g = argument

     h = sound argument

Exercise Three

1   Formal fallacy. From the premise 'All great artists have been slightly crazy', it doesn't follow that anyone who is slightly crazy will end up being a great artist.

2   Valid argument.

3   Formal fallacy. Speeding is not the only possible explanation of why you have been stopped by the police. So the conclusion cannot be deduced from the premises.

4   Formal fallacy. The first premise doesn't state that *only* philosophers are terrible writers. So the conclusion does not follow from the premises, since you could still be a terrible writer even though you weren't a philosopher (and, incidentally, you could still be an excellent writer even though you were a philosopher).

5   Valid argument (despite its false premise: dolphins *aren't* fish).

Exercise Four

1   deduction

2   induction

3   induction (provided that I haven't met every student)

4   deduction

5   deduction

Exercise Six

1   *Why, according to Rachels, do some people believe there to be a moral difference between active and passive euthanasia?*

Because they believe there is a moral difference between killing and letting die. Active euthanasia (which is seen as a form of killing) is then thought worse than passive euthanasia (which is considered a form of letting die).

2   *Which kind of euthanasia is Smith's case meant to parallel?*

The case of Smith is meant to be parallel to that of active euthanasia since Smith kills the child.

3   *Why has Rachels put inverted commas around the word 'accidentally'?*

The inverted commas around 'accidentally' are supposed to emphasize the fact that in Jones's case the child drowned not simply as the result of an accident but rather as a result of Jones choosing not to intervene once the initial accident had taken place. The point is that the drowning wasn't really an *accident* in the usual sense of the word.

4   *What sort of difference might the knowledge that Smith was mentally deranged make to our assessment of his case?*

We might want to argue that Smith's responsibility for his actions was in some way diminished as a result of his mental state. The extent to which we would be prepared to allow that his responsibility was diminished in such a case would depend very much on the precise nature of his derangement.

5   *Does Rachels believe there to be an important moral difference between the cases of Smith and Jones?*

Rachels aims to show that there is no significant moral difference between the cases of Smith and Jones.

Exercise Eight

Here is my summary of the passage. Don't worry if yours is slightly different, provided it includes the main points:

Non-human animals may one day be given the rights they deserve. Neither reasoning ability nor the ability to use language can be the basis for drawing a line between those creatures that merit rights and those that don't, since many animals have a greater ability to reason and are better at communicating than young children. But even if this weren't so, it wouldn't matter, because the only relevant ability is the ability to feel pain.

ANSWERS TO THE REVISION TEST

1   d

2   c

3   c

4   e

5   e

6   d

7   b

8   e

ACKNOWLEDGEMENT

Grateful acknowledgement is made to the following for permission to reproduce material in this unit:

Reprinted by permission of *The New England Journal of Medicine*: Rachels, J. (1975) 'Active and passive euthanasia', *The New England Journal of Medicine*, 292, pp.78–80, © 1975 Massachusetts Medical Society.

INDEX TO BLOCK 1

This index includes references to the Colour Plates and Plates in the *Illustration Book*; these are indicated by 'CPl' for Colour Plates, and 'Pl' for Plates.

AN INTRODUCTION TO THE HUMANITIES